WeightWatchers®

Exciting recipes with a touch of spice

Classic Curries

SIMON &
SCHUSTER
ILLUSTRATED

London · New York · Sydney · Toronto · New Delhi

A CBS COMPANY

If you would like to find out more about Weight Watchers and the **_ProPoints_** Plan, please visit: www.weightwatchers.co.uk

Ⓥ This symbol denotes a vegetarian recipe and assumes that, where relevant, free range eggs, vegetarian cheese, vegetarian virtually fat free fromage frais, vegetarian low fat crème fraîche and vegetarian low fat yogurts are used. Virtually fat free fromage frais, low fat crème fraîche and low fat yogurts may contain traces of gelatine so they are not always vegetarian. Please check the labels.

❄ This symbol denotes a dish that can be frozen. Unless otherwise stated, you can freeze the finished dish for up to 3 months. Defrost thoroughly and reheat until the dish is piping hot throughout.

Recipe notes

Egg size: Medium, unless otherwise stated.

Raw eggs: Only the freshest eggs should be used. Pregnant women, the elderly and children should avoid recipes with eggs that are not fully cooked or raw.

All fruits and vegetables: Medium, unless otherwise stated.

Stock: Stock cubes are used in recipes, unless otherwise stated. These should be prepared according to packet instructions.

Recipe timings: These are approximate and meant to be guidelines. Please note that the preparation time includes all the steps up to and following the main cooking time(s).

Microwaves: Timings and temperatures are for a standard 800 W microwave. If necessary, adjust your own microwave.

Low fat spread: Where a recipe states to use a low fat spread, a light spread with a fat content of no less than 38% should be used.

Low fat soft cheese: Where low fat soft cheese is specified in a recipe, this refers to soft cheese with a fat content of less than 5%.

ProPoints values: Should you require the **_ProPoints_** values for any of the recipes within this book, you can call Customer Services on 0845 345 1500 and we will provide you with the relevant information on a recipe-by-recipe basis. Please allow 28 days for us to provide you with this information.

WeightWatchers®

Exciting recipes with a touch of spice

Classic Curries

First published in Great Britain by Simon & Schuster UK Ltd, 2014
A CBS Company

Simon & Schuster Illustrated Books, Simon & Schuster UK Ltd,
First Floor, 222 Gray's Inn Road, London WC1X 8HB

www.simonandschuster.co.uk

Simon & Schuster Australia, Sydney
Simon & Schuster India, New Delhi

Weight Watchers Publications: Lucy Clements, Imogen Prescott, Nina McKerlie.

Recipes written by: Sue Ashworth, Sue Beveridge, Sara Buenfeld,
Tamsin Burnett-Hall, Cas Clarke, Siân Davies, Roz Denny, Nicola Graimes,
Becky Johnson, Kim Morphew, Joy Skipper, Penny Stephens and Wendy Veale
as well as Weight Watchers Leaders and Members.

Photography by: Iain Bagwell, Steve Baxter, Will Heap, Steve Lee, Lis Parsons,
Juliet Piddington and William Shaw.
Project editor: Sharon Amos.
Design and typesetting: Geoff Fennell.
Proofreading: Jane Bamforth.

Printed and bound in China.

A CIP catalogue record for this book is available from the British Library

ISBN 978-1-47113-166-0

10 9 8 7 6 5 4 3 2 1

Pictured on the title page: Lamb rogan josh p64.
Pictured on the Introduction: Prawn masala p92, Indian salad with flaked almonds p24,
Thai fried rice with toasted cashews p144.

Contents

Introduction

We all love curries and classic dishes such as Chicken Tikka Masala regularly top the polls as our favourite dish. Here we'll introduce you to a wide range of curries from across the globe – from Traditional Thai Curry to Malaysian Pork With Pineapple – as well as regional variations from India such as Beef Dopiaza with lots of onions and lentil-based Vegetable Dhansak. Many curries are vegetarian and we also give you tips on adding meat to various dishes to keep vegetarians and meat eaters satisfied at the same sitting. There are also delicious seafood curries, from Tandoori Prawns to Thai Green Curry with Cod. When a curry is a hot one, we'll warn you – and you'll find tips on how to reduce the heat, as well as how to boost the heat of milder dishes.

Alongside all the traditional accompaniments and side dishes you'd expect, from Cucumber Chutney to a yogurt and mint Raita, as well as classic Bombay Potatoes – all with far fewer calories than their take-away counterparts – you'll discover how to cook the perfect rice every time. And you'll find Indian chapatis and naan breads surprisingly easy to make at home. Finally, to finish off there are new takes on traditional Indian puddings and ice creams.

About Weight Watchers

For more than 40 years Weight Watchers has been helping people around the world to lose weight using a long term sustainable approach. Weight Watchers successful weight loss system is based on four tried and trusted principles:

- Eating healthily
- Being more active
- Adjusting behaviour to help weight loss
- Getting support in weekly meetings

Our unique *ProPoints* system empowers you to manage your food plan and make wise recipe choices for a healthier, happier you.

Buying spices

You're going to need a well-stocked spice cupboard to make these recipes. Follow these handy tips for the best-tasting, freshest spices.

Ground spices – check the dates on those in your cupboard and buy new jars or packets if necessary. If you live near an ethnic grocery or supermarket, buy from there instead of your usual supermarket. Prices can sometimes be lower and there will be a great choice. If possible, buy little and often, so that spices are as fresh as possible and keep them in a cool dark place. Replace them regularly if you don't use them all up.

Whole spices – if you want to grind your own spices, invest in a pestle and mortar or an electric spice grinder. The colour and aroma of ready-ground spices can fade – freshly ground ones have far more flavour. Toasting whole spices releases their aroma. If you are going to grind your own, toast them first by dry frying in a pan for a minute or two, but don't let them burn.

Curry and spice pastes – these handy ingredients are available in the ethnic food departments of large supermarkets and from specialist retailers. Don't be afraid to experiment.

Ready-prepared lemongrass, ginger and garlic – these are great as an emergency standby; use them when necessary.

Storing and freezing

Many curries store well in the fridge, but make sure you use them up within a day or two. Some can also be frozen. However, it is important to make sure you know how to freeze safely.

- Wrap any food to be frozen in rigid containers or strong freezer bags. This is important in order to stop foods contaminating each other or getting freezer burn.
- Label the containers or bags with the contents and date – your freezer should have a star marking that tells you how long you can keep different types of frozen food.
- Never freeze warm food – always let it cool completely first.
- Never freeze food that has already been frozen and defrosted.
- Freeze food in portions, then you can take out as little or as much as you need each time.

- Defrost what you need in the fridge, making sure you put anything that might have juices, such as meat, on a covered plate or in a container.

Shopping hints and tips

When you're going around the supermarket it's tempting to pick up foods you like and put them in your trolley without thinking about how you will use them. So, a good plan is to decide what dishes you want to cook before you go shopping, check your storecupboard and make a list of what you need. You'll save time by not drifting aimlessly around the supermarket picking up what you fancy.

We've added a checklist here for the spices and store cupboard ingredients you'll need. Just add fresh ingredients to your regular shop and you'll be ready to cook *Classic Curries.*

Storecupboard checklist

- [ ] almonds, ground, flaked and sliced
- [ ] apricots, canned
- [ ] apricots, dried ready-to-eat
- [ ] balti curry paste and powder
- [ ] bay leaves
- [ ] black mustard seeds
- [ ] beans, canned, various types
- [ ] cardamom pods
- [ ] cashew nuts
- [ ] chilli flakes, dried
- [ ] chilli powder
- [ ] chilli sauce
- [ ] Chinese five spice
- [ ] cinnamon, ground
- [ ] cinnamon sticks
- [ ] coconut, dessicated
- [ ] coconut essence
- [ ] coconut milk, reduced fat
- [ ] condensed milk, light, canned
- [ ] cooking spray, calorie controlled
- [ ] coriander seeds
- [ ] coriander, ground
- [ ] cornflour
- [ ] cumin, ground
- [ ] cumin, seeds

- [ ] curry (paste and powder)
- [ ] curry leaves
- [ ] evaporated milk, light, canned
- [ ] fenugreek, ground
- [ ] flour, plain
- [ ] fructose (or caster sugar)
- [ ] garam masala
- [ ] honey, clear
- [ ] icing sugar
- [ ] jalfrezi curry paste
- [ ] korma curry paste
- [ ] lentils, canned
- [ ] lentils, dried red
- [ ] lime leaves, dried
- [ ] mint sauce
- [ ] mustard (Dijon and wholegrain)
- [ ] nutmeg, ground
- [ ] oil (vegetable and olive)
- [ ] passata
- [ ] pineapple, canned in natural juice
- [ ] pistachios, shelled, unsalted
- [ ] poppy seeds
- [ ] pudding rice, dried
- [ ] rice, dried (basmati, brown basmati, jasmine and long grain)
- [ ] rogan josh curry powder

- [ ] saffron threads
- [ ] salt
- [ ] soy sauce
- [ ] spilt yellow peas
- [ ] star anise
- [ ] stem ginger in syrup
- [ ] stock cubes
- [ ] sultanas
- [ ] sweetcorn, canned
- [ ] tamarind paste
- [ ] tandoori spice mix
- [ ] Thai fish sauce
- [ ] Thai green curry paste
- [ ] Thai red curry paste
- [ ] tikka spice mix
- [ ] tikka masala curry paste
- [ ] tomato purée
- [ ] tomatoes, canned
- [ ] turmeric
- [ ] vanilla extract
- [ ] vindaloo curry paste
- [ ] vinegar (balsamic and wine)
- [ ] Worcestershire sauce
- [ ] yeast, active, dried

Starters and sides

Bombay potatoes

Serves 4
126 calories per serving
Takes 25 minutes

❄

450 g (1 lb) new potatoes,
    halved or quartered
3 garlic cloves, chopped
5 cm (2 inches) fresh root
    ginger, peeled and chopped
    finely
2 teaspoons ground coriander
1 teaspoon hot chilli powder
1 teaspoon ground turmeric
6 vine ripened tomatoes,
    de-seeded and chopped
1 tablespoon tomato purée
1 tablespoon lemon juice
calorie controlled cooking
    spray
2 teaspoons cumin seeds
4 cardamom pods, split
7 curry leaves
salt and freshly ground black
    pepper
coriander leaves, to serve

New potatoes in a spicy tomato sauce – without the high calorie count of your favourite take-away side dish.

1 Cook the potatoes in plenty of boiling water until tender, then drain and set aside.

2 Meanwhile, in a bowl, mix together the garlic, ginger, ground coriander, chilli, turmeric, fresh tomatoes, tomato purée and lemon juice, along with 125 ml (4 fl oz) water.

3 Spray a wok with the cooking spray and fry the cumin seeds, cardamom pods and curry leaves for 30 seconds. Stir in the spicy tomato mixture and stir-fry for 2 minutes over a medium-low heat.

4 Add the potatoes, turning them to coat them in the sauce, and cook, stirring occasionally, for 2 minutes. Season and serve sprinkled with coriander leaves.

Onion bhajees

Serves 2, makes 4 bhajees
55 calories per serving
Takes 15 minutes to prepare,
20 minutes to cook

calorie controlled cooking
spray
1 onion, sliced finely
50 g (1¾ oz) plain flour
4 tablespoons water
1 garlic clove, crushed
½ teaspoon ground turmeric
½ teaspoon ground cumin
½ teaspoon ground coriander
½ teaspoon chilli powder
salt and freshly ground black
pepper

This is another low-calorie version of a popular starter.

1 Preheat the oven to Gas Mark 7/220°C/fan oven 200°C.

2 Spray a non-stick frying pan with the cooking spray and fry the onion for about 8 minutes until very soft and brown.

3 Mix together all the other ingredients with 4 tablespoons of water to form a thick paste – if it is more dough-like, add a little more water. Now mix in the onions and stir well.

4 Divide the mixture into 4 equal portions and place each in a non-stick muffin tin. Bake in the preheated oven for 20 minutes.

5 Take the bhajees out and turn them upside down before returning to the oven for another 5 minutes. Serve warm.

Tip… Serve two bhajees per person with some low fat yogurt mixed with a little no-added-sugar mint sauce.

Cucumber chutney

Serves 4

15 calories per serving

Takes 10 minutes +
   20 minutes chilling

½ a medium cucumber, sliced
   very thinly into long strips
1 garlic clove, crushed
1 medium green chilli,
   de-seeded and chopped
   finely
1 tablespoon white wine
   vinegar
1 teaspoon sugar
a pinch of poppy seeds

*Tiny poppy seeds are used to provide flavour and decoration
in Indian dishes. They taste mild and slightly nutty. Here
they are used in a spicy but refreshing side dish.*

1 Put the cucumber into a sieve and press as much liquid out
of the strips as you can with the back of a wooden spoon.

2 Chop the cucumber strips and put them in a serving bowl.

3 Mix together the garlic, chilli, vinegar and sugar, and stir
until the sugar has dissolved.

4 Pour this mixture over the cucumber, sprinkle it with poppy
seeds and chill for at least 20 minutes before serving.

Bombay salad

Serves 2
238 calories per serving
Takes 15 minutes

175 g (6 oz) new potatoes,
  sliced
2 eggs
2 teaspoons black mustard
  seeds
75 g (2¾ oz) frozen petits pois,
  defrosted
1 small red onion, chopped
  finely
100 g (3½ oz) baby spinach
  leaves
½ small fennel bulb, trimmed
  and sliced finely
75 g (2¾ oz) cherry tomatoes,
  halved
2 teaspoons mild curry
  powder
2 tablespoons white wine
  vinegar
2 teaspoons Dijon mustard

*This warm salad is based on classic Bombay potatoes with
the addition of hard-boiled eggs and all topped with a mild
curry dressing.*

1 Bring a pan of water to the boil, add the potatoes, cover and
cook for 10 minutes until tender.

2 Meanwhile, put the eggs into a pan of cold water and bring
to the boil. Reduce the heat and simmer for 7 minutes.
Drain and plunge the eggs into cold water. Drain the potatoes,
reserving 3 tablespoons of the cooking water and return the
potatoes to the pan.

3 While the potatoes and eggs are cooking, put the mustard
seeds, petits pois, onion, spinach, fennel and cherry tomatoes
into a bowl and toss gently to combine. Divide between two
serving plates.

4 Peel the eggs and cut each in half. Mix together the curry
powder, wine vinegar, mustard and reserved cooking water.
Stir the mixture into the warm sliced potatoes. Top each salad
with the dressed potatoes and top with the egg halves.

Curried sweet potato and lentil soup

Serves 4

214 calories per serving

Takes 15 minutes to prepare,
15 minutes to cook

**calorie controlled cooking
spray**

1 onion, chopped finely

**1.2 litres (2 pints) hot
vegetable stock**

**1 green chilli, de-seeded and
chopped finely**

**2 teaspoons finely grated
fresh root ginger**

1 teaspoon ground cumin

**1 tablespoon medium curry
powder**

**400 g (14 oz) sweet potatoes,
cubed**

**100 g (3½ oz) red lentils,
rinsed and drained**

juice of ½ a lime or lemon

To serve

**4 tablespoons 0% fat Greek
yogurt**

**4 tablespoons chopped fresh
coriander**

*A delicious and delicately spiced soup that's quick and
easy to prepare.*

1 Heat a large, lidded saucepan and spray with the cooking
spray. Fry the onion for 1 minute, then add 2 tablespoons of
the stock and cook, stirring, for 3–4 minutes.

2 Stir in the chilli, ginger, cumin and curry powder and cook
for 1 minute, then mix in the sweet potatoes, lentils and
remaining stock. Bring to the boil, cover and simmer for
15 minutes or until the sweet potatoes and lentils are tender.

3 Transfer the soup to a liquidiser, or use a hand-held blender,
and blend until smooth, adding the lime or lemon juice. Return
to the pan and reheat if necessary. Serve with the yogurt and
coriander.

Tomato and coriander salad

Serves 2

15 calories per serving

Takes 5 minutes + 20 minutes
chilling

2 medium tomatoes

**½ tablespoon chopped fresh
coriander leaves**

a pinch of chilli powder

a pinch of sugar

½ tablespoon lemon juice

**salt and freshly ground black
pepper**

*Tomato and coriander complement each other beautifully –
serve this quick side dish with any curry.*

1 Slice one of the tomatoes into wedges. Finely chop the
second tomato.

2 Mix all the ingredients together in a bowl. Cover and chill
for 20 minutes before serving.

Roasted spiced chick peas

Serves 4
85 calories per serving
Takes 5 minutes to prepare,
 45 minutes to cook

**410 g can chick peas, drained
 and rinsed**
**1 tablespoon tandoori curry
 powder**
½ teaspoon ground turmeric
1 teaspoon dried chilli flakes
**calorie controlled cooking
 spray**
salt (optional)

*These tasty little nibbles make a great low calorie
alternative to crisps and nuts, and are very simple to make.*

1 Preheat the oven to Gas Mark 7/220°C/fan oven 200°C.

2 Tip the chick peas into a mixing bowl and add the tandoori
spice mix, turmeric and chilli flakes. Stir the chick peas until
coated in the spices.

3 Spray a large non-stick baking tray with the cooking spray.
Tip the chick peas on to the tray and spread them out in a
single layer.

4 Roast the chick peas in the oven for 40–45 minutes until
crisp and golden. Remove them from the oven and transfer to
a serving bowl. Season with salt if desired, before serving.

Variation... Instead of the tandoori curry powder, you could
use tikka curry powder, garam masala or korma spice mix.

Indian salad with flaked almonds

Serves 1
330 calories per serving
Takes 35 minutes

100 g (3½ oz) new potatoes,
  scrubbed and halved
125 g (4½ oz) small
  cauliflower florets
15 g (½ oz) flaked almonds
50 g (1¾ oz) canned chick
  peas, drained and rinsed
1 tablespoon chopped red
  onion
1 tomato, de-seeded and
  chopped
1 tablespoon chopped fresh
  coriander

For the dressing
1 tablespoon tamarind paste
2 tablespoons low fat natural
  yogurt
1 tablespoon finely chopped
  fresh root ginger
1 tablespoon lemon juice
a large pinch of ground cumin
salt and freshly ground black
  pepper

A fun way to serve this salad is on top of a crisp poppadum.

1 Bring a saucepan of water to the boil, add the potatoes and cook for 10 minutes or until tender. Drain, then cut into bite size pieces.

2 Meanwhile, put the cauliflower in a steamer basket over a saucepan of 2.5 cm (1 inch) gently boiling water and cook for 3–5 minutes until just tender. (If you don't have a steamer basket, bring a pan of water to the boil, add the cauliflower and cook until just tender.)

3 Put the almonds in a dry non-stick frying pan and toast over a medium-low heat for 2–3 minutes until light golden. Remove from the heat and leave to cool.

4 Mix together the ingredients for the dressing with 1 tablespoon of hot water and season.

5 Combine the potatoes, cauliflower and chick peas in a bowl then spoon the dressing over. Toss until coated then spoon on to a serving plate. Top with the red onion, tomato, coriander and flaked almonds. Serve immediately.

Tip… Tamarind is available as a paste or in a powdered or concentrated form. It's widely used in Asian and Middle Eastern food and gives a slightly sour flavour to curries, chutneys and soups. It is also a key ingredient in Worcestershire sauce.

Variation… Add 100 g (3½ oz) cooked, diced Quorn to the salad in step 4.

Raita

Serves 2

45 calories per serving

Takes 5 minutes

10 cm (4 inches) cucumber, halved, de-seeded and cubed finely

2 spring onions, chopped finely

2 teaspoons lemon juice

1 teaspoon mint sauce

125 g (4½ oz) low fat natural yogurt

salt and freshly ground black pepper

An excellent accompaniment for curry dishes, especially the hotter ones.

1 Mix all ingredients together and chill before serving.

Variation…You can also add some chopped fresh mint.

Saag aloo

Serves 1
155 calories per serving
Takes 20 minutes

calorie controlled cooking
spray
1 medium onion, sliced
110 g (4 oz) baby spinach
leaves
200 g (7 oz) potatoes, cooked
and cubed
2.5 cm (1 inch) fresh root
ginger, peeled and grated
1 garlic clove, chopped
1 medium green chilli, de-
seeded and chopped finely
1 teaspoon medium curry
powder
1 teaspoon poppy seeds
salt and freshly ground black
pepper

*Serve this spinach and potato dish instead of rice – it
also makes a delicious vegetarian curry on its own.*

1 Heat a non-stick pan and spray with the cooking spray.
Stirfry the onion for about 5 minutes until soft.

2 Add the remaining ingredients to the pan together with
2 tablespoons water. Stir until the spinach has wilted.

3 Heat gently until simmering, then cover the pan with a
tight-fitting lid and cook for 3 minutes or until the potatoes
have warmed through.

4 Season to taste, then serve.

Spicy samosas

Makes 8 samosas

165 calories per serving of 2 samosas plus sauce

Takes 20 minutes to prepare, 15 minutes to cook

❄ (samosas only, before cooking)

275 g (9½ oz) potatoes, peeled and diced

150 g (5½ oz) frozen mixed vegetables (e.g. carrots, green beans, peas and sweetcorn)

calorie controlled cooking spray

1½ teaspoons curry powder

4 x 45 g sheets of filo pastry

2 teaspoons mint sauce

150 g (5½ oz) low fat natural yogurt

These crisp, curried samosas can be served straight from the oven, or leave them to cool and pack them in your lunchbox or for a picnic.

1 Preheat the oven to Gas Mark 6/200°C/fan oven 180°C. Bring a lidded saucepan of water to the boil and add the potatoes. Cover and cook for 4 minutes. Add the mixed vegetables, replace the lid and cook for 3 minutes more. Drain the potatoes and vegetables in a colander.

2 Spray the saucepan with the cooking spray. Return the vegetables to the pan, mix in the curry powder and cook, stirring, for 1 minute. Tip on to a plate to cool.

3 Cut each sheet of filo in half lengthways to give eight long strips. Working with one strip at a time, spray with cooking spray and spoon one eighth of the filling on the top. Bring the top left corner across to the other side to make a triangle. Flip this over and over until you reach the bottom of the strip and the filling is completely enclosed. Place on a baking tray and spray with cooking spray. Repeat to make eight samosas in total.

4 Bake the samosas for 15 minutes until crisp and golden brown.

5 Stir the mint sauce into the yogurt and serve the sauce with 2 samosas per person.

Tikka potato wedges

Serves 4

98 calories per serving

Takes 10 minutes to prepare,
55 minutes to cook

500 g (1 lb 2 oz) potatoes,
unpeeled, scrubbed, halved
lengthways and cut into
wedges

calorie controlled cooking
spray

2 teaspoons tikka spice mix

salt and freshly ground black
pepper

*These potato wedges have a light, spicy coating and are
delicious served with the Raita on page 27.*

1 Preheat the oven to Gas Mark 7/220°C/fan oven 200°C.
Pat dry the potatoes with kitchen towel then put them in a
mixing bowl. Spray with the cooking spray, stirring the
potatoes as you do. Sprinkle with the tikka spice mix,
season and stir the potatoes again to coat them
in the spices.

2 Spray a large non-stick baking tray with the
cooking spray and arrange the potatoes on the
tray. Bake them for about 50–55 minutes,
turning twice, until golden.

Chicken and turkey

Chicken balti

Serves 2

225 calories per serving

Takes 15 minutes to prepare,
20 minutes to cook

**calorie controlled cooking
spray**

1 medium onion, sliced

**1 medium red pepper,
de-seeded and cut into thick
strips**

**2 x 150 g (5½ oz) skinless,
boneless chicken breasts,
cubed**

1 garlic clove, crushed

**2.5 cm (1 inch) fresh root
ginger, peeled and grated**

**1 medium green chilli, de-
seeded and chopped finely**

**1 teaspoon medium curry
powder**

**2 cardamom pods, crushed
slightly**

½ teaspoon cumin seeds

**3 tablespoons low fat plain bio
yogurt**

1 tablespoon lemon juice

**salt and freshly ground black
pepper**

**fresh coriander leaves, to
garnish**

*The balti originally came from Pakistan and has been
enthusiastically adopted by restaurants in Britain. Serve
with home-made Naan bread (see page 138).*

1 Heat a non-stick pan and spray with the cooking spray.
Stir-fry the onion and pepper for about 5 minutes until soft.

2 Add the chicken to the pan and cook for 2–3 minutes or until
brown on all sides.

3 Add all the other ingredients, except the coriander, to the
pan. Heat gently until simmering, then cover the pan with a
tight-fitting lid and cook for 15 minutes.

4 Remove the lid and cook for a few minutes more until the
sauce has reduced and thickened slightly.

5 Season to taste and serve garnished with coriander leaves.

Chicken tikka kebabs

Serves 4

215 calories per serving

Takes 30 minutes +
  10 minutes marinating

100 g (3½ oz) low fat natural
  yogurt
4 teaspoons tikka curry
  powder
¼ teaspoon hot chilli powder
  (optional)
1 garlic clove, crushed
juice of ¼ lime
4 x 150 g (5½ oz) skinless,
  boneless chicken breasts,
  each cut into 3 strips
calorie controlled cooking
  spray
salt and freshly ground black
  pepper

*Serve these tender marinated chicken pieces hot from the
grill – or the barbecue.*

1 Mix together the yogurt, curry powder, chilli powder (if
using), garlic and lime juice in a large shallow dish. Season.
Add the chicken and stir well until it is coated in the marinade.
Set aside for 10 minutes.

2 Preheat the grill to medium-hot and cover the grill pan with
foil. Thread the chicken strips on to 12 metal skewers, spray
with the cooking spray and grill for 5 minutes on each side until
cooked through. Serve three kebabs each with a lime wedge.

Tips... Add a sweetcorn and pepper salad by mixing
together 200 g (7 oz) canned sweetcorn, 1 cubed red
pepper, a handful of shredded lettuce leaves, 2 tablespoons
chopped fresh mint and a good squeeze of lime juice and
divide between four.

Serve with 1 medium pitta bread per person and the Raita
on page 27.

Chicken korma

Serves 4

522 calories per serving

Takes 20 minutes to prepare,
35 minutes to cook

❄ (without banana)

**calorie controlled cooking
spray**

**500 g (1 lb 2 oz) skinless,
boneless chicken breasts,
chopped into chunks**

1 large onion, chopped

**1 eating apple, peeled, cored
and chopped**

1 garlic clove, crushed

**2 tablespoons korma curry
paste**

**400 ml (14 fl oz) chicken or
vegetable stock**

25 g (1 oz) sultanas

250 g (9 oz) dried brown rice

1 tablespoon cornflour

**4 tablespoons low fat natural
yogurt**

1 banana

**salt and freshly ground black
pepper**

*The classic mild option on the curry menu reinvented here
with a low calorie creamy sauce.*

1 Spray a large lidded saucepan with the cooking spray.
Add the chicken, onion, apple and garlic and stir-fry for 2–3
minutes. Stir in the curry paste and cook for a few seconds.

2 Add the stock and sultanas. Bring up to the boil then reduce
the heat and simmer, partially covered, for 35 minutes. Stir
occasionally, adding a little more stock or water, if necessary.

3 Meanwhile, bring a pan of water to the boil. Add the rice and
cook according to the packet instructions until tender. Drain.

4 Just before serving, add 2 tablespoons of cold water to
the cornflour and stir to blend. Add the blended cornflour to
the curry, stirring until thickened. Add the yogurt and slice
in the banana, cooking gently for a few moments. Check the
seasoning and serve with the rice.

Fruity chicken curry

Serves 4

278 calories per serving

Takes 20 minutes to prepare,
20 minutes to cook

❄

**calorie controlled cooking
 spray**
100 g (3½ oz) lardons
1 onion, chopped
**4 x 165 g (5¾ oz) skinless,
 boneless chicken breasts,
 cut into bite size pieces**
1 teaspoon curry powder
1 teaspoon ground cumin
1 apple, cored and sliced
1 banana, sliced
4 plum tomatoes, chopped
250 ml (9 fl oz) chicken stock

*A fruity, great-tasting curry that goes well with plain boiled
rice (see page 142 for how to cook perfect rice every time).*

1 Heat a large saucepan, spray with the cooking spray and
add the lardons and onion. Cook for 2–3 minutes before adding
the chicken.

2 Brown the chicken and then sprinkle in the spices. Stir to
coat the chicken. Add the remaining ingredients and bring
to a simmer.

3 Simmer the curry for 15–20 minutes, then serve.

Chicken massalam

Serves 4

185 calories per serving

Takes 10 minutes to prepare +
30 minutes soaking, 1 hour
to cook

a pinch of saffron threads

**4 x 150 g (5½ oz) skinless,
boneless chicken breasts**

**salt and freshly ground black
pepper**

**a handful of coriander leaves,
to garnish**

For the sauce

juice of a lemon

**5 cm (2 inches) fresh root
ginger, peeled and grated**

1 garlic clove, crushed

½ cinnamon stick

**6 cardamom pods, crushed
slightly**

1 teaspoon ground turmeric

½ teaspoon salt

½ teaspoon cumin seeds

**150 g (5½ oz) low fat plain bio
yogurt**

*Massalam is another form of the word 'masala', which
refers to any combination of spices used in an Indian dish.
The saffron turns the chicken a lovely yellow colour. Serve
it with Tomato and Coriander Salad (see page 22).*

1 Soak the saffron threads in 2 tablespoons of hot water for
at least 30 minutes, reserving the soaking liquid.

2 Preheat the oven to Gas Mark 4/180°C/fan oven 160°C.
Place the chicken breasts in a single layer in a flame and
ovenproof lidded dish.

3 Mix the saffron and its soaking water with the other sauce
ingredients and pour over the chicken. Cover with a tight-fitting
lid and bake for 55 minutes.

4 Remove the chicken from the dish and set to one side,
keeping it warm while preparing the sauce.

5 Pour the cooking juices from the dish into a food processor
or liquidiser and whizz until smooth. Return to the dish and
warm through on the hob for a few minutes until the sauce
has reduced and thickened slightly.

6 Divide the sauce between four serving plates, and place a
chicken breast in the middle of each. Season to taste and serve
garnished with a few coriander leaves.

Chicken tikka masala

Serves 2

255 calories per serving

Takes 45 minutes + 20 minutes marinating (or overnight)

2 tablespoons low fat plain bio yogurt

1 tablespoon tandoori curry powder

1 tablespoon lemon juice

2 x 150 g (5½ oz) chicken breasts, cut into 8 pieces

fresh coriander, to garnish

For the masala sauce

calorie controlled cooking spray

1 medium onion, chopped

2 garlic cloves, crushed

2.5 cm (1 inch) fresh root ginger, grated

1 teaspoon medium-strength curry powder

½ teaspoon mild chilli powder

½ teaspoon cumin seeds

1 tablespoon tomato purée

15 g (½ oz) ground almonds

1 tablespoon lemon juice

1 tablespoon half-fat crème fraîche

Once voted the nation's favourite dish, chicken tikka masala is a combination of marinated spicy chicken in a medium hot sauce.

1 Mix together yogurt, tandoori spice, and lemon juice. Put the chicken pieces in a dish, pour the yogurt mix over and stir well. Cover the dish and put in the fridge to marinate for at least 20 minutes, but preferably 8–10 hours, if you have time.

2 When ready to cook, preheat the grill or griddle.

3 Heat a non-stick pan and spray with the cooking spray. Stir-fry the onion for about 8 minutes until soft and brown.

4 Add all the sauce ingredients to the pan, except the crème fraîche, together with 100 ml (3½ fl oz) water. Heat gently until simmering, then cover the pan with a tight-fitting lid and cook gently for 15 minutes.

5 Grill or griddle the chicken pieces for about 12-15 minutes, turning to cook on all sides, until just starting to blacken and the chicken is cooked through.

6 Remove the lid from the pan and heat the sauce for a few minutes longer until it has reduced and thickened. Stir in the crème fraîche and add the chicken pieces. Simmer gently for 15 minutes more before serving. Garnish with fresh coriander.

Tips… Serve with a salad of Iceberg lettuce, sliced onions and tomato wedges. Or serve with a portion of Saffron Rice (page 147) or a home-made Naan (page 138).

Tandoori powder is easy to make yourself. Use 1 teaspoon each of medium curry powder, turmeric and chilli powder.

Indian spiced chicken

Serves 4

370 calories per serving

Takes 25 minutes to prepare
  + 1 hour marinating,
  25 minutes to cook

❄

4 x 125 g (4½ oz) skinless,
  boneless chicken breasts

100 g (3½ oz) low fat natural
  yogurt

2 garlic cloves, crushed

½ teaspoon ground turmeric

1 teaspoon ground cumin

2 shallots, chopped very finely

2 tablespoons lemon juice

2 tablespoons chopped fresh
  coriander

½ teaspoon salt

225 g (8 oz) dried basmati rice

50 g (1¾ oz) frozen peas

2 tomatoes, de-seeded and
  diced

1 tablespoon chopped fresh
  mint

salt

4 lemon wedges, to serve

*Roasted marinated chicken served with a rice and
vegetable mix.*

1 Score the top of the chicken breasts and arrange them in
a shallow non metallic dish. Mix together the yogurt, garlic,
turmeric, cumin, shallots, lemon juice, coriander and salt.
Spoon this mixture over the chicken, mix well to coat each
breast, and then cover and leave to marinate for 1 hour.

2 Preheat the oven to Gas Mark 5/190°C/fan oven 170°C.
Line a baking tray with non-stick baking parchment and place
the marinated chicken breasts on it. Bake in the oven for 25
minutes.

3 Meanwhile, place the rice in a large saucepan with 600 ml
(20 fl oz) water, and bring to the boil. Reduce the heat, add the
peas and simmer for 12 minutes until the rice is tender. Drain
well. Stir the diced tomatoes and mint into the rice.

4 Spoon the rice on to warmed plates and top with a chicken
breast and a lemon wedge to squeeze over.

Tip… If you like hot curries, add a teaspoon of chilli
powder along with the other spices.

Tandoori chicken

Serves 1

290 calories per serving

Takes 30 minutes + 1 hour marinating or overnight

❄

175 g (6 oz) skinless, boneless chicken breast

calorie controlled cooking spray

a wedge of lime, to serve

For the marinade

3 tablespoons low fat natural yogurt

1 garlic clove, crushed

1 tablespoon finely grated fresh ginger

1 tablespoon tandoori curry powder

1 teaspoon ground turmeric

salt and freshly ground black pepper

For the tomato salad

1 tomato, de-seeded and diced

2 tablespoons lime juice

½ a red onion, sliced thinly

½ a mild green chilli, sliced thinly

1 tablespoon chopped fresh mint

Tandoori chicken takes its name from the clay oven it was traditionally cooked in, but it tastes just as good cooked in the oven at home.

1 Mix together the ingredients for the marinade in a shallow, non-metallic dish and season. Make three slashes diagonally across the chicken breast and place it in the dish. Spoon the marinade over the chicken, rubbing the paste into the cuts. Leave to marinate for at least 1 hour or preferably overnight, if you have time.

2 Preheat the oven to Gas Mark 7/220°C/fan oven 200°C. Spray a baking dish with the cooking spray and add the chicken. Roast in the oven for 20 minutes until the chicken is golden and cooked through with no trace of pink in the centre.

3 While the chicken is roasting, combine all the ingredients for the tomato salad in a bowl and season to taste. Serve the chicken hot with the salad and a wedge of lime to squeeze over.

Turkey Madras

Serves 2

215 calories per serving

Takes 10 minutes to prepare,
20 minutes to cook

❄

calorie controlled cooking
  spray
1 medium onion, chopped
300 g (10½ oz) turkey breast,
  diced
1 garlic clove, chopped finely
2.5 cm (1 inch) fresh root
  ginger, peeled and grated
1 medium green chilli, de-
  seeded and chopped finely
1 tablespoon medium curry
  powder
2 cardamom pods, crushed
  slightly
2 teaspoons chilli powder
1 teaspoon ground coriander
½ teaspoon cumin seeds
200 ml (7 fl oz) chicken stock
salt and freshly ground black
  pepper

Madras curries tend to be synonymous with heat. This version is not too hot, though you could serve it with a cooling Raita (see page 27) just in case.

1 Heat a non-stick pan and spray with the cooking spray. Stir-fry the onion for about 5 minutes until soft.

2 Add the turkey to the pan and cook for 2–3 minutes or until brown on all sides.

3 Add the remaining ingredients, heat gently until simmering, then cover the pan with a tight-fitting lid and cook for 15 minutes.

4 Remove the lid and cook for 2–3 minutes more until the sauce has reduced and thickened slightly.

5 Season to taste, then serve.

Variation… This dish can also be made with cubed chicken breast instead of turkey.

Traditional Thai curry

Serves 4
165 calories per serving
Takes 20 minutes to prepare,
15 minutes to cook

calorie controlled cooking spray
**500 g (1 lb 2 oz) skinless,
boneless chicken thighs, fat
removed, cut into bite size
pieces**
300 ml (10 fl oz) chicken stock
**1 tablespoon Thai fish sauce
or Worcestershire sauce**
**2 dried kaffir lime leaves or
the zest of 2 limes**
**2 medium aubergines,
quartered, then sliced and
placed in salted water**
**a small bunch of fresh
coriander, chopped**

For the spice paste
**2 small bird's eye chillies,
de-seeded and chopped (or 1
teaspoon dried chilli flakes)**
**a stalk of lemongrass,
chopped finely (or
1 teaspoon ready-prepared)**
**2.5 cm (1 inch) fresh root
ginger, peeled and chopped
finely**
4 garlic cloves, sliced
3 shallots, sliced

*You can buy ready-made Thai curry paste, but home-made
is fresher and tastier.*

1 First make the spice paste by grinding all the ingredients in
a mill on the food processor or in a pestle and mortar.

2 Heat a large frying-pan or wok and spray with the cooking
spray. Fry the spice paste for about 30 seconds until aromatic,
then add the chicken pieces and stir-fry for 2 minutes until the
chicken changes colour. Add the stock, fish or Worcestershire
sauce, and lime leaves and bring to the boil.

3 Rinse and drain the aubergine slices and add to the curry.
Simmer for 15 minutes until just cooked through. Sprinkle with
fresh coriander and serve.

Tip… Why not serve with Perfectly Cooked Rice (see
page 142)?

Beef, lamb and pork

Beef dopiaza

Serves 2

266 calories per serving

Takes 20 minutes to prepare,
   1 hour to cook

❄

200 g (7 oz) onions, chopped
   finely

4 cm (1½ inches) fresh root
   ginger, peeled and chopped

2 garlic cloves, chopped

calorie controlled cooking
   spray

1 teaspoon cumin seeds

250 g (9 oz) lean beef brisket,
   visible fat removed, and
   chopped into small cubes

2 teaspoons garam masala

1 teaspoon ground turmeric

1 large carrot, sliced thickly

200 ml (7 fl oz) vegetable
   stock

salt and freshly ground black
   pepper

*Dopiaza recipes feature lots of onions. This dish is
simmered gently until the beef is tender.*

1 Place half of the onion, the ginger, garlic and 3 tablespoons
of water in a food processor, or use a hand-held blender, and
whizz to make a paste.

2 Heat a medium, lidded, non-stick saucepan and spray with
the cooking spray. Add the remaining onions, cover and cook
for 5 minutes, stirring occasionally. Add the cumin seeds and
beef and cook for about 3 minutes until browned all over. Stir
in the garam masala and turmeric.

3 Add the blended onion paste, carrot and stock and bring
to the boil. Stir, then reduce the heat, cover and simmer for
about 1 hour or until the beef is very tender. Add a little water
if the sauce becomes too dry – the meat should be coated in
a thick sauce. If the sauce is too thin at the end of the cooking
time, remove the lid and simmer until reduced. Season to taste
before serving.

Tip… Serve with Perfectly Cooked Rice (page 142).

Oriental beef with butternut squash

Serves 4

274 calories per serving

Takes 25 minutes to prepare,
1 hour 35 minutes to cook

❄

500 g (1 lb 2 oz) lean beef
brisket, visible fat removed,
and diced

calorie controlled cooking
spray

2 onions, sliced

1 star anise

1 teaspoon Chinese five spice

5 cm (2 inches) fresh root
ginger, peeled and sliced
finely

100 ml (3½ fl oz) fresh orange
juice

5 tablespoons dark soy sauce

1 red chilli, de-seeded and
chopped (optional)

450 g (1 lb) butternut squash,
peeled, de-seeded and cut
into large, bite size pieces

salt and freshly ground black
pepper

*In this aromatic beef stew recipe, the meat is cooked
slowly in a sauce flavoured with orange juice, Chinese
five spice and star anise.*

1 Heat a large lidded flame and ovenproof dish. Spray the
beef with the cooking spray and add half the meat to the pan,
searing it until browned all over. Using a slotted spoon, remove
the beef and set to one side. Repeat with the remaining beef.

2 Once all the beef has been seared, put the onions in the pan,
spray with the cooking spray, and cook over a medium heat for
4 minutes, stirring occasionally. Add the star anise, Chinese
five spice and ginger, then stir-fry for a minute.

3 Pour in 400 ml (14 fl oz) water, the orange juice, soy sauce,
and chilli, if using. Stir and then add the beef. Bring to the boil,
then reduce the heat, cover, and simmer for 1 hour.

4 Add the squash and cook for a further 30 minutes, partially
covered, or until the squash and beef are tender and the sauce
is reduced and thickened. If the sauce is too thin, remove the
lid and cook for a few more minutes. Season to taste before
serving.

Lamb chana masala

Serves 1
369 calories per serving
Takes 30 minutes
❄

2 teaspoons tikka spice mix

100 g (3½ oz) lean, boneless lamb leg steak, visible fat removed

calorie controlled cooking spray

1 small onion, chopped

1 large garlic clove, chopped

1 teaspoon ground cumin

1 cm (½ inch) fresh root ginger, peeled and chopped finely

1 tablespoon balti curry paste

200 g (7 oz) canned chopped tomatoes

50 g (1¾ oz) canned chick peas, drained and rinsed

75 g (2¾ oz) spinach leaves, tough stalks removed

2 teaspoons lime juice

salt and freshly ground black pepper

Curries don't have to take long to cook, as you'll see with this simple recipe.

1 Rub the tikka spice mix all over the lamb. Season and set aside.

2 Heat a lidded non-stick saucepan and spray with the cooking spray. Add the onion, cover and cook for 5 minutes, stirring occasionally.

3 Add the garlic, cumin and ginger then stir in the curry paste. Cook for a minute, then add the chopped tomatoes and chick peas. Bring the tomato mixture up to the boil, then reduce the heat and simmer, partially covered, for 5 minutes. Stir in the spinach and lime juice, season, and cook for another 5 minutes.

4 While the curry is cooking, heat a lidded non-stick frying pan. Spray the lamb with the cooking spray and cook for 2–3 minutes on each side, depending on the thickness of the lamb, until browned and cooked to your liking. Remove from the heat, cover and leave to rest for a few minutes.

5 Slice the lamb on the diagonal and serve on top of the chick pea curry.

Easy spiced lamb

Serves 4
376 calories per serving
Takes 40 minutes
❄

200 g (7 oz) dried brown
basmati rice, rinsed

125 g (4½ oz) fine green
beans, trimmed

125 g (4½ oz) small
cauliflower florets

calorie controlled cooking
spray

1 onion, chopped

3 large garlic cloves, chopped

2.5 cm (1 inch) fresh root
ginger, peeled and chopped
finely

1 large courgette, diced

350 g (12 oz) lean diced lamb,
visible fat removed

50 g (1¾ oz) dried apricots,
chopped into small pieces

2 tablespoons garam masala

½ teaspoon chilli powder

salt and freshly ground black
pepper

An easy curry that combines rice, vegetables, dried
apricots and lamb with a simple spice mix.

1 Put the rice in a lidded saucepan and cover with 450 ml
(16 fl oz) water. Bring to the boil, then reduce the heat to its
lowest setting, cover, and simmer for 25 minutes until the
water is absorbed and the grains are tender. Set the pan aside
for 5 minutes, covered, then remove the lid and leave the rice
to cool slightly.

2 Bring about 2.5 cm (1 inch) of water to the boil in a lidded
pan. Put the green beans and cauliflower in a steamer basket
and place it over the pan. Cover and cook for 5 minutes until
al dente. Alternatively, bring a small amount of water to the
boil and cook the vegetables for 5 minutes, then drain. Refresh
under cold running water then set aside.

3 Heat a large lidded wok or non-stick frying pan. Spray with
the cooking spray and stir-fry the onion over a medium heat
for 4 minutes. Add the garlic, ginger and courgette and stir-fry
for 3 minutes. Next, add the lamb and stir-fry for a further
3 minutes until browned.

4 Add the apricots and spices, stir, and then add the green
beans, cauliflower, rice and 5 tablespoons of water. Stir until
combined, then cover with a lid and heat through for 5 minutes.
Season before serving.

🅥 **Variation...** Replace the lamb with four hard boiled eggs.
Halve the eggs and place on top of the cooked rice just
before serving.

Lamb saag

Serves 4

285 calories per serving

Takes 25 minutes

❄

calorie controlled cooking spray

2 medium onions, chopped

400 g (14 oz) lean lamb neck fillet, diced

2 garlic cloves, crushed

5 cm (2 inches) fresh root ginger, peeled and grated

1 medium green chilli, de-seeded and chopped finely

1 tablespoon medium curry powder

1 teaspoon chilli powder

1 teaspoon ground coriander

2 x 400 g cans chopped tomatoes

225 g (8 oz) baby spinach leaves

salt and freshly ground black pepper

Saag refers to the spinach in this medium-strength curry.

1 Heat a non-stick pan and spray with the cooking spray. Stirfry the onions for about 5 minutes until soft.

2 Add the diced lamb to the pan and cook for 2–3 minutes until brown on all sides.

3 Add all the other ingredients to the pan, except the spinach. Heat gently until simmering, then cover the pan with a tight-fitting lid and cook for 5 minutes.

4 Remove the lid, add the spinach and continue to cook for about 2–3 minutes or until the spinach has wilted into the curry and the sauce has reduced and thickened slightly. Season to taste, then serve.

Tip… Serve with Saffron Rice (page 147).

Lamb rogan josh

Serves 4

315 calories per serving

Takes 20 minutes to prepare,
  1 hour to cook

❄

calorie controlled cooking
  spray
2 onions, sliced
500 g (1 lb 2 oz) lean lamb leg
  steak, cubed
1 garlic clove, crushed
1 teaspoon grated fresh root
  ginger or ready-prepared
  fresh ginger
1½ tablespoons rogan josh
  curry powder
400 g can chopped tomatoes
2 carrots, sliced
1 lamb or chicken stock cube,
  dissolved in 150 ml (5 fl oz)
  boiling water
2 tablespoons tomato purée
1 tablespoon chopped fresh
  coriander
salt and freshly ground black
  pepper

Rogan josh is a rich, aromatic Indian curry with a distinctive red colour.

1 Heat a large saucepan, and spray it with the cooking spray. Add the onions and cook, stirring, for 3–4 minutes until they are lightly browned.

2 Add the lamb, a handful at a time, and cook over a medium high heat until it is all sealed and browned. Add the garlic, ginger and rogan josh curry powder and cook, stirring, for 1 minute.

3 Add the chopped tomatoes, carrots, stock, tomato purée and chopped coriander to the pan. Season with a little salt and black pepper and bring to the boil. Reduce the heat to low, then cover and simmer for about 1 hour, or until the lamb is very tender.

4 Check the seasoning, adding a little more salt and pepper, if necessary.

Tips... Serve with Perfectly Cooked Rice (page 142) and a refreshing Indian salad known as kachumba. Roughly chop a couple of tomatoes, half a red onion and 10 cm (4 inch) cucumber. Mix in a de-seeded and finely chopped large fresh green chilli and a couple of tablespoons of chopped fresh coriander. Add a squeeze of lime or lemon juice, and season with salt and pepper.

Lamb and apricot curry

Serves 4

375 calories per serving

Takes 15 minutes to prepare,
1 hour to cook

❄

calorie controlled cooking spray

350 g (12 oz) lean lamb leg steaks, cut into chunks

2 tablespoons balti curry paste

1 large onion, chopped

600 ml (20 fl oz) lamb or vegetable stock

2 tablespoons tomato purée

1 red pepper, de-seeded and cut into chunks

100 g (3½ oz) green beans, trimmed and halved

200 g (7 oz) cauliflower, broken into florets

411 g can apricot halves in natural juice, drained and halved

50 g (1¾ oz) frozen peas

2 tablespoons chopped fresh coriander

150 g (5½ oz) dried rice

1 tablespoon cornflour

4 tablespoons low fat natural yogurt

Fruit and meat are often partnered in curries. Here apricots add a sweet contrast to the lamb steaks.

1 Heat a large lidded saucepan and spray with the cooking spray. Add the lamb, letting it sear and brown before turning over. Cook for 3–4 minutes until browned on all sides.

2 Add the curry paste, onion, stock and tomato purée. Bring to the boil, then reduce the heat. Cover and simmer for 40 minutes.

3 Add the pepper, green beans, cauliflower and apricots to the curry. Simmer for a further 20 minutes, or until the cauliflower is tender, then add the peas and coriander.

4 Meanwhile, bring a pan of water to the boil and cook the rice according to the packet instructions. Drain thoroughly.

5 Blend the cornflour with 2 tablespoons of cold water, add it to the curry and stir until thickened. Cook for 1–2 minutes. Serve the curry with the rice and a tablespoon of yogurt each.

Tandoori lamb kebabs with minted rice

Serves 1
442 calories per serving
Takes 25 minutes
❄

- 60 g (2 oz) dried brown basmati rice
- 1 teaspoon chopped fresh mint
- 150 ml (5 fl oz) boiling water
- 75 g (2¾ oz) low fat natural yogurt
- 1½ teaspoons tandoori curry powder
- 1 teaspoon lemon juice
- 125 g (4½ oz) lean lamb leg steak, trimmed of all fat and cut into bite size pieces
- ½ red or green pepper, de-seeded and cut into bite size pieces
- 75 g (2¾ oz) button mushrooms
- calorie controlled cooking spray

The tandoori spice flavours the lamb without the need for marinating, but if you do have time to marinate for half an hour or so, the lamb will become even more flavoursome and tender.

1 Place the rice and half the mint in a lidded saucepan with the boiling water. Bring to the boil, stir once, then cover and cook, undisturbed, for 25 minutes over a very low heat until all the water has been absorbed and the rice is tender.

2 Meanwhile, mix 50 g (1¾ oz) of the yogurt with the tandoori curry powder, lemon juice and remaining mint. Stir the lamb and peppers into the spiced yogurt, along with the mushrooms. Preheat the grill to medium.

3 Thread the lamb and vegetables on to two metal skewers. Spray with the cooking spray and grill for 12 minutes, turning halfway through.

4 Stir the remaining yogurt into the hot rice and serve with the kebabs.

🅥 **Variation…** Try making tandoori vegetable kebabs by leaving out the lamb and increasing the mushrooms to 150 g (5½ oz) and adding a small courgette, cut into chunky slices.

Tip… While cooking, why not prepare a meal for another night at the same time? Double the quantity of meat, cover in the marinade and pop half straight into the freezer in a freezer bag. The meat will then marinate while defrosting.

Pork kofta in red curry sauce

Serves 2

278 calories per serving

Takes 20 minutes to prepare
+ 30 minutes chilling,
20 minutes to cook

❄

200 g (7 oz) extra lean pork
mince

2 large spring onions, chopped
finely

3 large garlic cloves, crushed

2.5 cm (1 inch) fresh root
ginger, peeled and grated

1 egg, lightly beaten

salt and freshly ground black
pepper

1 tablespoon chopped fresh
coriander, to garnish

For the red curry sauce

calorie controlled cooking spray

1 small onion, chopped finely

1 tablespoon Thai red curry
paste

100 ml (3½ fl oz) vegetable
stock

100 ml (3½ fl oz) reduced fat
coconut milk

2 tablespoons canned
chopped tomatoes

1 tablespoon lime juice

*Kofta are meatballs, here simmered in a tomato and
coconut milk sauce.*

1 Mix together the mince, spring onions, two of the garlic
cloves, half of the ginger and the egg in a bowl. Season, then
using wet hands, form into eight balls, each about the size of a
walnut. Arrange on a plate then cover and chill in the fridge for
30 minutes.

2 Meanwhile, to make the sauce, heat a large lidded saucepan,
spray with the cooking spray and fry the onion for 5 minutes,
stirring occasionally until softened. Add a little water if the
onion starts to stick. Add the remaining garlic and ginger then
the red curry paste, and cook, stirring, for a minute.

3 Pour in the vegetable stock, coconut milk and chopped
tomatoes and stir until combined. Bring to the boil then reduce
to simmering point. Arrange the meatballs in the pan and
spoon over the sauce. Partially cover the pan and simmer the
meatballs for 15 minutes, turning occasionally, until cooked
through.

4 Using a slotted spoon, remove the meatballs from the pan
and arrange on two plates. Keep warm. Stir the lime juice into
the sauce and then cook, uncovered, for another 5 minutes
until thickened. Season to taste then spoon the sauce over the
meatballs. Scatter with the coriander before serving.

Tip… Serve this curry with steamed green beans and
Perfectly Cooked Rice (page 142).

Spiced pork with mint raita

Serves 2

123 calories per serving

Takes 15 minutes
+ 30 minutes – 1 hour
marinating

1 tablespoon Thai red curry
paste

a stalk of lemongrass,
chopped

1 garlic clove, chopped

1 tablespoon low fat natural
yogurt

125 g (4½ oz) lean pork fillet,
trimmed of all fat

calorie controlled cooking
spray

wedges of lime, to serve

For the mint raita

5 tablespoons low fat natural
yogurt

5 cm (2 inches) cucumber,
cubed

3 tablespoons chopped fresh
mint

¼ teaspoon cumin seeds

salt and freshly ground black
pepper

Pork fillet is marinated in Thai spices and seared under the grill.

1 Put the red curry paste, lemongrass, garlic and yogurt in a food processor or blender and process until combined. Spread the mixture over the pork fillet and marinate in the fridge for 30 minutes to an hour.

2 Meanwhile mix together the ingredients for the mint raita in a bowl and season to taste.

3 Preheat the grill to medium hot and line the pan with foil. Spray the foil with the cooking spray and grill the pork for 4 minutes on each side.

4 Serve with plenty of mint raita.

Tip... Serve with Perfectly Cooked Rice (page 142).

Malaysian pork with pineapple

Serves 6
233 calories per serving
Takes 50 minutes

1 large onion, quartered
700 ml (1¼ pints) chicken stock
1 tablespoon ground coriander
1 teaspoon ground turmeric
½ teaspoon white pepper
2 star anise
1 cinnamon stick
1 cm (½ inch) fresh root
  ginger, peeled and chopped
2 garlic cloves, sliced
1 cucumber, peeled,
  de-seeded and sliced thickly
1 tablespoon salt
4 strips lime zest
227 g can pineapple chunks
  in natural juice
400 ml can reduced fat
  coconut milk
2 large red peppers, de-
  seeded and cut into strips
1–2 red chillies, de-seeded
  and sliced
1 tablespoon Thai fish sauce
30 g pack fresh coriander,
  leaves and stalks separated
  and both chopped
500 g (1 lb 2 oz) lean pork
  fillet, sliced into rounds

A fragrant oriental dish like this is ideal for entertaining friends. The recipe contains quite a lot of salt, but don't be alarmed – it's only used to draw the moisture out of the cucumber, then thoroughly rinsed off.

1 Put the onion in the food processor with the chicken stock and whizz until really smooth. Tip into a large lidded pan and bring to the boil. Reduce the heat, add the ground and whole spices, ginger and garlic, then cover the pan and leave to simmer for 20 minutes.

2 Meanwhile, toss the cucumber with the salt and set aside to allow the salt to draw out the excess water.

3 When the onion mixture has simmered for 20 minutes, stir in the lime zest, the juice from the pineapple and the coconut milk, then stir in the peppers, chillies, fish sauce, chopped coriander stalks and pork. Cover the pan and cook gently for 10 minutes.

4 Rinse the cucumber to remove all traces of salt, then stir it into the pan with the remaining coriander, and the pineapple. Cook for just a minute to warm the pineapple, then serve.

Pork jalfrezi

Serves 4
185 calories per serving
Takes 30 minutes
❄

calorie controlled cooking spray
2 onions, chopped
2 red peppers, de-seeded and chopped
1 tablespoon tomato purée
300 g (10½ oz) pork escalopes, cubed
1 green pepper, de-seeded and sliced thinly
2 garlic cloves, crushed
5 cm (2 inches) fresh root ginger, peeled and grated
1 green chilli, de-seeded and chopped finely
1 tablespoon medium curry powder
1 teaspoon chilli powder
1 teaspoon cumin seeds
500 g (1 lb 2 oz) passata
1 tablespoon chopped fresh coriander
salt and freshly ground black pepper

Jalfrezi dishes are spicy, stir-fried curries. They are also cooked quickly so the meat needs to be cut into small pieces in order for it to cook properly.

1 Heat a lidded non-stick frying pan and spray with the cooking spray. Stir-fry the onions and red peppers for about 8 minutes until the peppers are soft and the onion is brown.

2 Put the onion and red pepper mixture into a food processor or liquidiser. Add the tomato purée and whizz until smooth. Set aside.

3 Heat the non-stick frying pan and spray again with the cooking spray. Stir-fry the pork and green pepper for 5–10 minutes until brown.

4 Return the onion and pepper purée to the pan and add all other ingredients, except the seasoning and coriander. Heat gently until simmering; then cover the pan with the lid and cook for 10 minutes.

5 Remove the lid and cook for 2–3 minutes more until the sauce is reduced and thickened slightly.

6 Season to taste, stir in the coriander and serve.

Variation… Instead of pork, use 3 x 150 g (5½ oz) skinless, boneless chicken breasts, cut into bite size pieces. Cook them for 15 minutes at step 4.

Fish and seafood

Fish fillets with curry sauce

Serves 2

245 calories per serving

Takes 25 minutes +
  30 minutes soaking

**2 x 200 g (7 oz) white fish
  fillets e.g. cod or haddock**

**a small pinch of saffron
  threads**

**2 tablespoons warm skimmed
  milk**

a small pinch of chilli powder

**salt and freshly ground black
  pepper**

For the curry sauce

150 ml (5 fl oz) skimmed milk

15 g (½ oz) low fat spread

15 g (½ oz) plain flour

1 teaspoon curry powder

½ teaspoon ground turmeric

*This is more of a colonial Indian dish than a traditional one,
but delicious all the same.*

1 Preheat the oven to Gas Mark 6/200°C/ fan oven 180°C.
Soak the saffron threads in the skimmed milk for at least
30 minutes, reserving the soaking liquid.

2 Place the fish fillets on a piece of foil on a baking sheet. Pour
the saffron and its soaking liquid over the fish and season with
a little chilli powder, salt and freshly ground black pepper. Wrap
the foil loosely around the fish to make a parcel and bake for
20 minutes.

3 After 15 minutes make the sauce by mixing all the
ingredients in a small non-stick pan. Heat gently until
simmering, then cook for 2–3 minutes, stirring frequently.

4 Unwrap the fish fillets and serve with the sauce.

Tip... Serve with steamed green beans.

Red Thai fish curry

Serves 4
200 calories per serving
Takes 30 minutes
❅

600 ml (20 fl oz) fish stock

2 tablespoons red Thai curry
paste

1 tablespoon Thai fish sauce

finely grated zest and juice of
a lime

2 lemongrass stalks, sliced
thinly

100 g (3½ oz) fine green
beans, halved

350 g (12 oz) salmon fillets,
skinned and cubed

225 g (8 oz) cherry tomatoes,
halved

3 tablespoons chopped fresh
coriander

*In Thailand a curry made in this way without coconut milk
is often referred to as a jungle curry.*

1 Pour the fish stock into a large saucepan, stir in the curry
paste, fish sauce, lime zest and juice and lemongrass. Bring
to the boil and allow the mixture to bubble for 5 minutes.

2 Add the green beans and cook for 5 minutes. Stir in the
salmon and tomatoes and cook for a further 5 minutes, or until
the salmon is cooked and flakes easily.

3 Scatter the coriander over the top and then ladle the curry
into bowls to serve.

Tips... Most major supermarkets now sell fresh
lemongrass stalks in the fresh herb section. To prepare
lemongrass, peel away the outer skin and slice the rest
very thinly. You can also buy ready-prepared lemongrass.

Serve with boiled jasmine rice – follow the recipe for
Perfectly Cooked Rice (page 142).

Thai green curry with cod

Serves 4

160 calories per serving

Takes 10 minutes to prepare,
   15 minutes to cook

❄

300 ml (10 fl oz) reduced fat
   coconut milk

150 ml (5 fl oz) fish stock

1 garlic clove, crushed

4 kaffir lime leaves

1 tablespoon Thai fish sauce

2 tablespoons Thai green
   curry paste

4 shallots, halved

125 g (4½ oz) fine green
   beans, halved

350 g (12 oz) cod fillet,
   skinned and cubed

125 g (4½ oz) cherry
   tomatoes, halved

2 tablespoons chopped fresh
   coriander

Chunks of cod are quickly cooked in a fragrant coconut milk sauce.

1 Place the coconut milk, fish stock, garlic, lime leaves, fish sauce and curry paste in a pan and bring to the boil. Add the shallots. Allow the mixture to bubble for 10 minutes.

2 Add the green beans and cod and cook for a further 5 minutes. Toss in the tomatoes and coriander and simmer for a further 2–3 minutes. Serve at once.

Tips… Thai cooking uses fish sauce a little like Chinese cooking uses soy sauce. Take care when adding, as it is very salty. Add a little and taste. Then add more if required.

Look out for reduced fat coconut milk; it's a useful addition to your storecupboard when you're trying to lose weight.

Fish korma

Serves 1
250 calories per serving
Takes 15 minutes

calorie controlled cooking
  spray
½ medium onion, chopped
**200 g (7 oz) haddock fillet,
  cubed**
1 garlic clove, crushed
**2.5 cm (1 inch) fresh root
  ginger, peeled and grated**
**100 g (3½ oz) low fat plain bio
  yogurt**
2.5 cm (1 inch) cinnamon stick
**1 cardamom pod, crushed
  slightly**
½ teaspoon ground turmeric
¼ teaspoon cumin seeds
¼ teaspoon chilli powder
**salt and freshly ground black
  pepper**
**1 medium green chilli, cut into
  rings, to garnish (optional)**

*Cardamoms come in three different colours, each with
a slightly different flavour. In a traditional korma, brown
cardamoms are used for their mildly astringent taste.*

1 Heat a non-stick pan and spray with the cooking spray.
Fry the onion for about 5 minutes until soft.

2 Add the rest of the ingredients to the pan, stir and heat
gently until simmering, then cover the pan with a tight-fitting
lid and cook for 6–7 minutes until the fish is cooked through.

3 Season to taste and garnish with rings of fresh green chilli,
if using.

Variation... Make a prawn korma by substituting 100 g
(3½ oz) cooked large tiger prawns for the fish. Make the
curry sauce first, then stir in the prawns and heat through
before serving.

Tip... Serve the curry with spinach garnished with some
skinned, chopped tomato.

Indian tuna curry

Serves 4

315 calories per serving

Takes 20 minutes to prepare,
20 minutes to cook

❄

500 g (1 lb 2 oz) tuna steaks

calorie controlled cooking
spray

1 large onion, sliced

1 garlic clove, crushed

1 medium courgette, sliced

3 medium tomatoes, skinned
and chopped

1 small aubergine, chopped

400 g can chopped tomatoes

400 g can chick peas, drained
and rinsed

1 teaspoon ground cumin

1 tablespoon chopped fresh
coriander

2 tablespoons mild curry paste

salt and freshly ground black
pepper

To serve

fresh coriander sprigs

4 lime or lemon wedges

*A wonderful, fragrant fish curry made with filling fresh
tuna steaks.*

1 Rinse the fish, chop it into large chunks, and set aside.

2 Heat a large frying pan or wok and spray with the cooking
spray. Add the onion and garlic and sauté over a medium
heat for 2 minutes. Add the courgette, fresh tomatoes and
aubergine, and cook, stirring, for a further 2–3 minutes.

3 Add the canned tomatoes, chick peas, cumin, chopped
coriander and curry paste. Stir well and bring to the boil.
Reduce the heat and simmer for 15 minutes.

4 Add the fish chunks and stir them in gently. Cook for another
5–6 minutes, until the fish is cooked and looks opaque. Taste,
adding salt and pepper, if needed.

5 Ladle the fish curry into four serving bowls and garnish with
coriander sprigs. Serve with the lime or lemon wedges.

Tip… Serve with Perfectly Cooked Rice (page 142).

Variation… Try replacing the tuna with swordfish.

King prawn saag

Serves 2
160 calories per serving
Takes 25 minutes

calorie controlled cooking spray

1 onion, chopped

1 garlic clove, crushed

2.5 cm (1 inch) fresh root ginger, peeled and grated

½ tablespoon medium curry powder

1 teaspoon ground coriander

½ teaspoon chilli powder

400 g can chopped tomatoes

200 g (7 oz) raw king prawns, heads and shells removed, de-frosted if frozen and patted dry on kitchen paper

100 g (3½ oz) baby spinach leaves

salt and freshly ground black pepper

This is another quick-and-easy curry – it's made with prawns and is delicious served with naan bread and a chutney of your choice.

1 Heat a lidded non-stick frying pan and spray with the cooking spray. Stir-fry the onion for about 5 minutes until soft.

2 Add all the ingredients to the pan, except the prawns and spinach, and heat them gently until simmering; then cover the pan with a tight-fitting lid and cook for 10 minutes.

3 Remove the lid, add the prawns and spinach and stir for 4–5 minutes or until the prawns are pink and cooked through and the spinach has wilted.

4 Season to taste and serve.

Fish Madras

Serves 2
240 calories per serving
Takes 25 minutes

**2 x 200g (7 oz) cod fillets,
each cut into 4 pieces**
a sprinkling of chilli powder
**salt and freshly ground black
pepper**

For the sauce
**calorie controlled cooking
spray**
1 medium onion, chopped
2 garlic cloves, crushed
**5 cm (2 inches) fresh root
ginger, peeled and grated**
**1 medium green chilli, de-
seeded and chopped finely**
**2 tablespoons medium curry
powder**
2 teaspoons chilli powder
1 teaspoon ground coriander
½ teaspoon cumin seeds
200 ml (7 fl oz) fish stock

*This curry is quite hot so serve with a raita (see page 27)
to cool you down.*

1 Preheat the grill or griddle. Season the fish with a sprinkling
of chilli powder, salt and pepper.

2 Cook under the grill for 10–15 minutes, depending on the
thickness of the fillets, turning once during cooking. To check
the fish is cooked through, lift the skin with the point of a sharp
knife. If the flesh has turned white it is ready.

3 Meanwhile, make the sauce. Heat a non-stick pan and spray
with the cooking spray. Stir-fry the onion for about 5 minutes
until soft.

4 Add the rest of the sauce ingredients to the pan and heat
gently until simmering, then cover the pan with a tight-fitting
lid and cook for 5 minutes more.

5 Remove the skin from the cooked fish and discard. Gently
mix the fish with the sauce and serve immediately.

Prawn masala

Serves 1
340 calories per serving
Takes 20 minutes

1 teaspoon sunflower oil
1 small onion, chopped finely
1 garlic clove, crushed
½ teaspoon black onion seeds (see Tips)
1½ teaspoons hot curry powder
2 medium tomatoes, halved and grated (see Tips)
2 teaspoons tomato purée
125 g (4½ oz) peeled raw tiger prawns
3 drops of coconut extract

To serve
1 tablespoon desiccated coconut
freshly chopped coriander

Coconut extract is a clever way of introducing depth of flavour to a recipe, without adding any of the calories usually associated with coconut products. You can find it in the baking section at the supermarket, with the food colourings and flavourings. It is very concentrated so only add a drop at a time so as not to overdo it.

1 Heat the oil in a saucepan, add the onion and cook for 3 minutes until golden.

2 Add the garlic and spices, followed by the grated tomato, tomato purée and 100 ml (3½ fl oz) water. Simmer for 8 minutes until slightly reduced.

3 Stir in the prawns and the coconut essence and cook for 3 minutes, stirring occasionally, until the prawns are pink and cooked through.

4 Toast the desiccated coconut by heating it in a dry non-stick pan for about 2 minutes, shaking occasionally, until it starts to brown.

5 Serve the prawn masala garnished with the toasted coconut and fresh coriander.

Tips… Black onion seeds are also known as kalonji and are usually available from the spice section in the supermarket, as well as from Asian food stores. Grating tomato is a quick and effective way of using tomato flesh without having to worry about skinning it first.

Tandoori prawns

Serves 2

318 calories per serving

Takes 35 minutes +
  marinating + chilling

**300 g (10½ oz) frozen raw
  prawns with shells,
  de-frosted**

4 plain poppadums

¼ Iceberg lettuce, chopped

lemon wedges, to serve

For the marinades

juice of a lemon

2 garlic cloves, crushed

**5 cm (2 inches) fresh root
  ginger, peeled and grated**

**4 tablespoons low fat plain bio
  yogurt**

**1 tablespoon half fat crème
  fraîche**

**1 tablespoon tandoori curry
  powder**

For the raita

¼ cucumber, diced finely

**125 g (4 oz) low fat plain bio
  yogurt**

**1 tablespoon fresh coriander
  leaves, chopped**

**salt and freshly ground black
  pepper**

*Two marinades give the prawns a real depth of flavour in
this classic curry.*

1 Remove the main shells from the prawns and de-vein,
leaving the tails intact.

2 Make the first marinade by combining half the lemon juice
with the garlic and ginger in a bowl. Add the prawns, mix well
to coat and leave for 15 minutes.

3 Use a sieve to drain the prawns and marinade. Pat away
any excess moisture from the prawns with kitchen towel.

4 In a clean bowl, mix the rest of the lemon juice with the
remaining marinade ingredients; add the prawns and leave
to marinate in the fridge for 2–10 hours.

5 Mix all the raita ingredients together. Season. Chill until
required. Soak four wooden skewers in water for 20 minutes.

6 When ready to cook, preheat the grill or griddle to a
medium heat. Cook the poppadums according to the packet
instructions.

7 Divide the prawns between the skewers and use any excess
marinade to baste them. Grill them for about 5 minutes, or until
they have turned pink and are cooked through.

8 Serve two skewers each on a bed of Iceberg lettuce with
the raita. Garnish with the lemon wedges and serve with the
poppadums.

Mixed seafood curry

Serves 4
185 calories per serving
Takes 25 minutes

**calorie controlled cooking
  spray**
2 onions, chopped finely
2 garlic cloves, crushed
**5 cm (2 inches) fresh root
  ginger, peeled and grated**
**350 g (12 oz) skinned cod
  fillet, cut into bite size
  pieces**
**150 g (5 oz) 0% fat Greek
  yogurt**
**150 g (5 oz) low fat plain bio
  yogurt**
**1 tablespoon medium-strength
  curry powder**
1 teaspoon ground turmeric
**1 red chilli, de-seeded and
  chopped finely**
**250 g (9 oz) cooked mixed
  seafood selection, drained
  and dried on kitchen paper**
**salt and freshly ground black
  pepper**

*This dish comes from eastern Bengal and is delicious with
Cucumber Chutney (page 17) and plain basmati rice.*

1 Heat a non-stick saucepan, spray with the cooking spray
and cook the onions until soft but still uncoloured – about
4 minutes.

2 Add all the ingredients except the mixed seafood selection.
Bring up to a gentle heat, cover and cook for 5 minutes.
Uncover and add the seafood. Continue to cook until the
seafood has been heated through and the fish is completely
cooked. Do not overcook or the seafood will toughen.

3 Season and serve.

Thai red curry with prawns

Serves 2
185 calories per serving
Takes 15 minutes

225 g (8 oz) butternut squash,
  de-seeded and diced
100 g (3½ oz) green beans, cut
  into thirds
calorie controlled cooking
  spray
200 g (7 oz) raw peeled tiger
  prawns
1 tablespoon Thai red curry
  paste
100 ml (3½ fl oz) reduced fat
  coconut milk
juice of ½ a lime, plus wedges
  to serve
salt and freshly ground black
  pepper
fresh coriander, to garnish

Add a scattering of freshly chopped coriander to this Thai curry for an authentic finishing touch.

1 Add the diced butternut squash to a pan of boiling water. Cook for 4 minutes then add the green beans and cook for 4 minutes more. Drain the vegetables.

2 Spray a non-stick saucepan with the cooking spray, then fry the prawns with the curry paste for 2 minutes. Pour in the coconut milk, then add the drained vegetables and simmer for 1 minute.

3 Add the lime juice and seasoning to taste, just before serving. Garnish with fresh coriander and serve with lime wedges.

Vegetarian

Cauliflower vindaloo

Serves 2
241 calories per serving
Takes 25 minutes

calorie controlled cooking spray
½ a small onion, sliced finely
2 tablespoons vindaloo curry paste
1 red chilli, de-seeded and chopped finely
½ teaspoon ground ginger
1 cinnamon stick
1 tablespoon cider vinegar
300 ml (10 fl oz) hot vegetable stock
300 g (10½ oz) cauliflower, cut into small florets
125 g (4½ oz) potatoes, cubed
150 g (5½ oz) passata
50 g (1¾ oz) frozen peas

If you like things hot, this is a recipe for you. To reduce the heat, simply use a medium or mild curry paste instead.

1 Heat a wide, lidded, non-stick saucepan and spray with the cooking spray. Cook the onion for 3 minutes until beginning to soften.

2 Add the curry paste, chilli, ginger, cinnamon, cider vinegar, stock, cauliflower and potato. Bring to the boil, then reduce the heat, cover and simmer for 10 minutes.

3 Add the passata and peas and bring back to a simmer. Cook for 3 minutes until the sauce has thickened. Remove the cinnamon stick and discard it. Serve immediately.

Tips... This could serve 4 as a very tasty veggie side dish, for 120 calories per serving.

For a main meal, serve with two standard plain poppadums per person, some cooked spinach and a tomato, cucumber and red onion salad.

Chick pea and pepper curry

Serves 2
235 calories per serving
Takes 20 minutes

calorie controlled cooking spray
1 red pepper, de-seeded and chopped roughly
1 yellow pepper, de-seeded and chopped roughly
1 tablespoon medium curry powder
230 g can chopped tomatoes
100 g (3½ oz) low fat natural yogurt
410 g can chick peas, rinsed and drained
salt and freshly ground black pepper
2 tablespoons chopped fresh coriander (optional)

This colourful vegetarian curry is quick to make – and very tasty.

1 Spray a non-stick saucepan with the cooking spray and fry the peppers for 4 minutes until slightly browned.

2 Stir in the curry powder and cook for 30 seconds to develop the flavour, then mix in the chopped tomatoes, yogurt and chick peas. Add seasoning, cover the pan and simmer for 10 minutes.

3 Stir in the coriander, if using, just before serving.

Tip… Serve this flavoursome curry with brown rice (see Perfectly Cooked Rice, page 142), or spoon it over two medium size 225 g (8 oz) jacket potatoes.

Creamy aubergine curry

Serves 4

147 calories per serving

Takes 25 minutes to prepare,
20 minutes to cook

❄ (paste only)

For the paste

2 red chillies, de-seeded and chopped roughly

2 garlic cloves, chopped

2 tablespoons chopped fresh coriander leaves

½ teaspoon ground coriander

½ teaspoon ground cumin

2 kaffir lime leaves, shredded

½ small onion, chopped roughly

2 cm (¾ inch) fresh root ginger, peeled and chopped

For the curry

2 aubergines, weighing approx 450 g (1 lb), cut lengthways into thin slices

calorie controlled cooking spray

4 tomatoes on the vine, halved

400 ml can reduced fat coconut milk

A creamy, satisfying curry with a spicy kick. You can turn down the heat by reducing the number of chillies.

1 Place all the ingredients for the paste in a food processor and blend until smooth. You may need to add 1–2 tablespoons of water.

2 Heat a griddle pan or non-stick frying pan until hot. Spray the aubergine slices with the cooking spray and cook for 1–2 minutes until beginning to char. You may have to do this in batches.

3 Lightly coat a deep frying pan with the cooking spray and heat until hot. Add the paste and stir-fry for 1 minute. Add the tomatoes and cook for 2 minutes before adding the aubergines and coconut milk. Simmer for 20 minutes before serving.

Tip… Make double the quantity of paste and freeze half for another day.

Creamy root vegetable curry

Serves 4

450 calories per serving

Takes 40 minutes

calorie controlled cooking
  spray

1 onion, chopped

300 g (10½ oz) swede,
  chopped

200 g (7 oz) parsnips, chopped

200 g (7 oz) potatoes, chopped

2 large carrots, sliced

2 teaspoons curry powder

600 ml (20 fl oz) vegetable
  stock

350 g (12 oz) basmati rice

175 g (6 oz) low fat fromage
  frais

salt and freshly ground black
  pepper

*Spicy but not too hot, this curry will become a firm
vegetarian favourite.*

1 Heat a non-stick pan and spray with the cooking spray.
Fry the onion for 2–3 minutes. Add the remaining vegetables,
cover the pan and, over a very low heat, let them sweat for
4–5 minutes.

2 Stir in the curry powder, then pour in the stock. Simmer for
15–20 minutes, or until the vegetables are tender.

3 Meanwhile, cook the rice in a pan of boiling, salted water
according to packet instructions until al dente. Drain and keep
warm.

4 Take out two ladlefuls of vegetables and a little stock. Place
these in a food processor with the fromage frais and blend until
smooth. Return to the pan, stir well and check the seasoning.
Serve with the rice.

Lentil and vegetable curry

Serves 2

320 calories per serving

Takes 10 minutes to prepare,
  30 minutes to cook

This dish combines lentils and vegetables – including okra, a popular Indian veg – for a filling vegetarian curry.

1 Heat a large saucepan and spray with the cooking spray. Gently fry the onion and garlic for 5 minutes. Stir the curry powder, coriander seeds and chilli sauce into the onion, stirring well, then add the lentils, tomatoes and cauliflower. Cover and simmer gently for 15 minutes.

2 Meanwhile cook the rice according to the instructions on the packet.

3 After cooking the curry for 15 minutes, stir in the okra, cover the pan and continue to cook for another 10 minutes.

4 Stir in the mango chutney and squeeze the lemon juice over the curry, to taste. Season to taste and serve with the rice.

calorie controlled cooking
  spray
1 onion, sliced
1 garlic clove, crushed
½ tablespoon curry powder
1 teaspoon crushed coriander
  seeds or ground coriander
½ teaspoon chilli sauce
400 g can lentils, drained
400 g can chopped tomatoes
200 g (7 oz) cauliflower,
  separated into small florets
60 g (2 oz) dried rice
100 g (3½ oz) okra, sliced
40 g (1½ oz) mango chutney
½ a lemon, quartered
salt and freshly ground black
  pepper

Egg curry

Serves 2

415 calories per serving

Takes 10 minutes to prepare,
   20 minutes to cook

2 large eggs

100 g (3½ oz) dried long grain
   rice

1 tablespoon chopped fresh
   parsley or coriander

1 teaspoon poppy seeds

1 onion, sliced

1 large garlic clove, crushed

1 tablespoon ginger purée

1 large fresh green chilli,
   finely chopped

1 teaspoon sunflower oil

1 teaspoon mild or medium
   curry powder

230 g can chopped tomatoes

150 g (5½ oz) low fat plain bio
   yogurt

1 teaspoon plain flour

salt and freshly ground black
   pepper

2 tablespoons coarsely grated
   carrot, to serve

Lightly spicy and aromatic, this is a simple curry with a tangy touch.

1 Hard boil the eggs for 8 minutes, then cool them under cold running water. Peel and cut them into quarters. Set aside.

2 At the same time as cooking the eggs, boil the rice in lightly salted, boiling water according to the pack instructions. Drain the rice, then mix in the parsley or coriander and poppy seeds. Keep the rice mixture warm.

3 Put the onion, garlic, ginger purée, chilli and oil in a medium size saucepan with 3 tablespoons of water and heat until the mixture sizzles. Sauté gently for 5 minutes and then mix in the curry powder and cook for 1 minute.

4 Stir in the chopped tomatoes, 100 ml (3½ fl oz) of water and seasoning. Add the egg quarters to the pan. Simmer for 5 minutes.

5 Blend together the yogurt and flour and stir this mixture into the pan. Heat through, but do not boil. Check the seasoning. Divide the rice mixture between two serving plates and spoon the egg curry on top. Sprinkle with the grated carrot and serve.

Tips… Serve the curry as a main meal with chopped fresh tomatoes.

Coarsely grated carrot makes a colourful and healthy garnish if you have no fresh herbs for chopping.

Variation… Substitute 100 g (3½ oz) Quorn pieces for the eggs.

Indian sambhar

Serves 4

292 calories per serving

Takes 20 minutes to prepare,
15-20 minutes to cook

½ teaspoon mustard seeds

½ teaspoon cumin seeds

½ teaspoon dried chilli flakes

6 curry leaves

2 teaspoons desiccated
coconut

4 teaspoons vegetable oil

225 g (8 oz) red lentils, rinsed
and drained

½ teaspoon ground turmeric

425 ml (15 fl oz) vegetable
stock

4 tomatoes, chopped

450 g (1 lb) mixed vegetables,
such as okra, courgettes,
cauliflower, carrots, squash,
etc, diced

a bunch of fresh coriander,
chopped

2 garlic cloves, sliced thinly

salt and freshly ground black
pepper

*Spicy lentils are combined with mixed vegetables in this
dish from southern India.*

1 In a medium size non-stick saucepan fry the first five
ingredients with 2 teaspoons of the oil until the coconut
browns. Mix in the lentils, turmeric, stock, tomatoes and
seasoning and bring to the boil, then reduce the heat to low.

2 Cover and simmer until the lentils are mushy, about 15–20
minutes. Add the vegetables and cook until al dente. Stir in the
coriander.

3 Meanwhile heat the remaining 2 teaspoons of oil in a small
pan and fry the garlic until golden. Pour the garlic over the
cooked curry and fold together, then serve.

Masala vegetable curry

Serves 4
189 calories per serving
Takes 30 minutes

❄

300 g (10½ oz) sweet potato, cubed

calorie controlled cooking spray

2 onions, grated

3 cardamom pods, split

1 teaspoon yellow mustard seeds

1–2 teaspoons hot chilli powder, according to taste

1 tablespoon garam masala

2.5 cm (1 inch) fresh root ginger, peeled and chopped finely

4 garlic cloves, crushed

2 carrots, sliced thinly

150 g (5½ oz) chestnut mushrooms, halved

400 g can chopped tomatoes

300 ml (10 fl oz) vegetable stock

175 g (6 oz) frozen peas

140 g (5 oz) frozen leaf spinach

salt and freshly ground black pepper

All the taste of a masala sauce but with vegetables rather than meat.

1 Steam the sweet potato until tender.

2 Meanwhile, spray a medium size, heavy-based saucepan with the cooking spray. Add the onions and fry, stirring frequently, for 4 minutes until golden. Add the cardamom pods, mustard seeds, ground spices, ginger, garlic, carrots and mushrooms. Fry, stirring constantly, for 2 minutes.

3 Pour in the chopped tomatoes and vegetable stock and bring to the boil. Reduce the heat and simmer, covered, for 10 minutes, stirring occasionally.

4 Add the sweet potato, peas and spinach, then cook, uncovered, for a further 3–5 minutes. If the sauce is too watery, cook for slightly longer. Season and serve.

Tip... Serve with Perfectly Cooked Rice (page 142).

Mushroom curry

Serves 2

139 calories per serving

Takes 30 minutes

calorie controlled cooking spray

2 onions, sliced

300 g (10½ oz) mixed mushrooms (e.g. button, chestnut, oyster), sliced thickly or halved, depending on size

2 garlic cloves, crushed

2 teaspoons medium curry powder

½ teaspoon cumin seeds

3 tablespoons tomato purée

4 tablespoons low fat plain bio yogurt

½ teaspoon ground fenugreek (optional)

salt and freshly ground black pepper

Use whatever mushrooms are in season or on offer for this satisfying vegetarian dish.

1 Heat a non-stick pan and spray with the cooking spray. Stir-fry the onions for about 8 minutes until soft and brown.

2 Reduce the heat, add the rest of the ingredients to the pan and heat gently until the mushrooms start to release their juices. Cover the pan with a tight-fitting lid and simmer for 10 minutes, stirring regularly.

3 Remove the lid and continue cooking for a minute or two, then season to taste and serve.

Potato masala

Serves 4
141 calories per serving
Takes 25 minutes

400 g (14 oz) waxy new
  potatoes, halved
calorie controlled cooking
  spray
½ a small onion sliced finely
2 garlic cloves, crushed
5 dried curry leaves
1 teaspoon black mustard
  seeds
2 tablespoons tikka masala
  curry paste
2 large tomatoes on the vine,
  de-seeded and diced
150 g (5½ oz) low fat natural
  yogurt
salt and freshly ground black
  pepper

Curry leaves are very popular in South Indian cookery and give this dish a real burst of curry flavour.

1 Bring a pan of water to the boil, add the potatoes, cover and simmer for 15 minutes.

2 Meanwhile, heat a wide non-stick saucepan until hot and spray with the cooking spray. Add the onion, garlic, curry leaves and mustard seeds and cook for 3–4 minutes until beginning to soften. Add the curry paste and tomatoes and cook for a further minute.

3 Gradually stir in the yogurt, a spoonful at a time until it forms a thick sauce. Drain the potatoes and fold through the masala sauce, stirring gently until combined. Season to taste and serve immediately.

Potato, spinach and cauliflower curry

Serves 4
198 calories per serving
Takes 25 minutes

**calorie controlled cooking
  spray**
1 onion, sliced thinly
2 garlic cloves, crushed
**2 tablespoons medium curry
  powder**
1 teaspoon black onion seeds
400 g can chopped tomatoes
**200 ml (7 fl oz) hot vegetable
  stock**
**500 g (1 lb 2 oz) potatoes,
  cubed**
**400 g (14 oz) cauliflower, cut
  into small florets**
**½ teaspoon ground turmeric
  (optional)**
**100 g (3½ oz) baby spinach
  leaves**
**100 g (3½ oz) low fat natural
  yogurt**

*Adding turmeric to the potatoes and cauliflower gives them
a lovely golden hue.*

1 Heat a non-stick saucepan until hot and spray with the
cooking spray. Add the onion and cook for 5 minutes until
softened and starting to brown, adding a splash of water if it
starts to stick. Add the garlic, curry powder and black onion
seeds. Cook for 1 minute, stirring. Mix in the tomatoes and
stock and simmer for 5 minutes.

2 Meanwhile, bring a pan of water to the boil and add the
potatoes, cauliflower and turmeric, if using. Cook for 6 minutes
or until tender. Drain and stir into the curry sauce. Cook gently
for 5 minutes.

3 Mix in the spinach and cook until just wilted, then stir in the
yogurt to give a marbled effect just before serving.

Tip… If you don't have any black onion seeds, use cumin
seeds or brown mustard seeds instead.

Vegetable dhansak

Serves 4

264 calories per serving

Takes 20 minutes to prepare,
25 minutes to cook

150 g (5½ oz) red lentils,
rinsed and drained

2.5 cm (1 inch) fresh root
ginger, peeled, sliced thinly
and cut into matchsticks

4 garlic cloves, sliced

2 large onions, chopped
roughly

2 green chillies, sliced
(de-seeded if preferred)

1 cinnamon stick

2 bay leaves

1 aubergine, cut into large
chunks

300 g (10½ oz) potatoes,
cubed

1 teaspoon ground cumin

2 teaspoons ground coriander

½ teaspoon ground turmeric

2 tablespoons tomato purée

1 vegetable stock cube

150 g (5½ oz) baby spinach
leaves

*Dhansak-style curries are based on lentils and this version
is delicious.*

1 Add the lentils to a large lidded pan with the ginger, garlic,
onions, chillies, cinnamon stick, bay leaves and aubergine. Add
1 litre (1¾ pints) cold water and bring to the boil. Cover and
leave to simmer for 10 minutes.

2 Remove the pan from the heat and stir in the potatoes,
ground spices, tomato purée and stock cube. Return to the
heat, cover again and leave to cook for a further 15 minutes
until the vegetables are tender and the lentils are pulpy.

3 Turn off the heat and stir in the spinach leaves, allowing
them to wilt in the heat – there is no need to cook them.
Season to taste and serve.

Tip… Serve with a tablespoon of mango chutney and
a Weight Watchers mini plain naan per person or with
Perfectly Cooked Rice (page 142).

Thai green vegetable curry

Serves 2
142 calories per serving
Takes 35 minutes

75 g (2¾ oz) fine green beans, trimmed

calorie controlled cooking spray

250 g (9 oz) aubergine, sliced and quartered

2 tablespoons Thai green curry paste

300 ml (10 fl oz) vegetable stock

100 ml (3½ fl oz) reduced fat coconut milk

2.5 cm (1 inch) fresh root ginger, peeled and chopped finely

60 g (2 oz) baby corn

1 courgette, sliced diagonally

75 g (2¾ oz) chestnut mushrooms, halved

2 tablespoons chopped fresh coriander

salt and freshly ground black pepper

Aubergine slices turn this fragrant and creamy coconut curry into a filling dish.

1 Bring about 2.5 cm (1 inch) of water to the boil in a lidded pan. Put the green beans in a steamer basket and place it over the pan. Cover and steam for 5 minutes until almost cooked. Alternatively, bring a small amount of water to the boil and cook the beans for 5 minutes then drain. Refresh the beans under cold running water. Set aside.

2 Meanwhile, heat a large, lidded non-stick saucepan. Spray with the cooking spray and stir-fry the aubergine for 7 minutes until softened. Add a little water if it starts to stick.

3 Spray the pan again with the cooking spray, add the curry paste and cook, stirring, for 1 minute. Pour in the stock and stir until combined, then add the coconut milk, ginger, baby corn, courgette and mushrooms.

4 Bring to the boil, reduce the heat and simmer, partially covered, for 5–8 minutes until the sauce has reduced and thickened. Season and stir in the green beans and 1 tablespoon of the coriander. Heat through and serve sprinkled with the remaining coriander and some black pepper.

Tip... Serve with jasmine rice – follow the recipe for Perfectly Cooked Rice (page 142).

Sweet potato balti

Serves 4

201 calories per serving

Takes 30 minutes

500 g (1 lb 2 oz) sweet potato, peeled and halved lengthways, then sliced into half moons

calorie controlled cooking spray

400 g can chopped tomatoes with onion

1 garlic clove, crushed

2 tablespoons balti curry powder

150 ml (5 fl oz) hot vegetable stock

410 g can butter beans, drained and rinsed

1 red chilli, sliced

75 g (2¾ oz) frozen chopped spinach

2 tablespoons chopped fresh coriander

Caramelised sweet potatoes are stirred into a spicy chilli and bean sauce at the last minute.

1 Put the sweet potato on a heatproof plate and microwave on high for 5 minutes. Or bring a pan of water to the boil and cook the sweet potatoes for 10 minutes.

2 Heat a wide non-stick frying pan and spray with the cooking spray. Transfer the sweet potato to the pan and cook for 20 minutes, turning over about halfway through when starting to caramelise.

3 Meanwhile, put the chopped tomatoes, garlic, curry powder, stock, butter beans, chilli and frozen spinach into a saucepan. Bring to the boil and simmer for 5–10 minutes. Add the sweet potato and coriander and stir to combine. Serve immediately.

Tip… Serve with Perfectly Cooked Rice (page 142), 2 tablespoons low fat natural yogurt mixed with fresh mint and cucumber and a leafy green salad per person.

Yellow pea and tofu curry

Serves 4

329 calories per serving

Takes 20 minutes to prepare
+ 30 minutes marinating,
40 minutes to cook

Ⓥ ❄ (curry only)

2 tablespoons balti curry paste

2 tablespoons lime juice

250 g (9 oz) firm tofu, patted
dry and cut into 8 long slices

200 g (7 oz) dried yellow split
peas

calorie controlled cooking
spray

1 large onion, chopped

2.5 cm (1 inch) fresh root
ginger, peeled and grated

1 teaspoon cumin seeds

1 teaspoon mustard seeds

1 teaspoon ground turmeric

2 teaspoons ground coriander

1 large red chilli, halved
lengthways

2 carrots, cubed

300 ml (10 fl oz) vegetable
stock

100 ml (3½ fl oz) reduced fat
coconut milk

salt and freshly ground black
pepper

fresh coriander, to garnish

Yellow split peas make an economical and filling curry. They're easy to use, as they don't need to be pre-soaked. The tofu is marinated in spices and served on the curry.

1 Mix together the curry paste and lime juice with 1 tablespoon of warm water, then season. Add the tofu, turn to coat it, then leave to marinate for 30 minutes.

2 Put the split peas in a colander and rinse under cold running water. Tip them into a medium lidded saucepan, cover with plenty of water and bring up to the boil. Reduce the heat, partially cover the pan, and simmer for 40 minutes until tender. Skim off any foam that rises to the surface, topping up with more water if necessary. Drain the split peas and set aside.

3 Meanwhile, preheat the oven to Gas Mark 4/180°C/fan oven 160°C. Spray a large, lidded, non-stick saucepan with the cooking spray and cook the onion gently for 10 minutes, adding a splash of water if it starts to stick, until softened and golden. Stir in the ginger and spices and cook for another minute.

4 Spray a roasting tin with the cooking spray then roast the tofu for 20 minutes, turning halfway through.

5 Tip the split peas into the saucepan of onion and spices, along with the chilli, carrots and stock. Season and bring to the boil, then reduce the heat and simmer for 15 minutes, partially covered, until the vegetables are tender. Stir in the coconut milk and half of the fresh coriander. Simmer, partially covered, for another 5 minutes until warmed through.

6 Serve the curry in shallow bowls. Top with the tofu and sprinkle with the coriander.

Vegetable balti

Serves 2
220 calories per serving
Takes 30 minutes

1 small cauliflower, cut into
  florets
1 carrot, cut into bite size
  pieces
calorie controlled cooking
  spray
1 onion, finely chopped
4 cardamom pods
2 bay leaves
4 garlic cloves, crushed
8 cm (3 inches) fresh root
  ginger, peeled and grated
2 tablespoons curry powder
300 g (10½ oz) canned
  chopped tomatoes
300 ml (10 fl oz) vegetable
  stock
200 g (7 oz) frozen peas
150 g (5½ oz) frozen spinach
salt and freshly ground black
  pepper

*This delicately spiced curry uses a mix of fresh and frozen
vegetables.*

1 Bring a saucepan of water to the boil, add the cauliflower
and carrot and cook for about 2–3 minutes until just tender.
Drain and set aside.

2 Meanwhile, heat a lidded saucepan and spray with the
cooking spray. Cook the onion for 5 minutes, stirring
occasionally and adding a splash of water if it starts to stick,
then add the cardamom, bay leaves, garlic and ginger and cook
for another minute. Stir in the curry powder.

3 Add the tomatoes and stock and bring to the boil. Reduce
the heat and simmer for 5 minutes. Add the cooked cauliflower
and carrot and simmer, partially covered, for 7 minutes, stirring
occasionally. Stir in the peas and spinach and cook, uncovered,
for another 3 minutes or until the sauce has reduced and
thickened. Remove the bay leaves, season and serve.

Rice and bread

Almond-topped biryani

Serves 4

340 calories per serving

Takes 30 minutes to prepare, 40 minutes to cook

For the biryani

600 g (1 lb 5 oz) mixed vegetables, sliced

250 g (9 oz) dried basmati rice

550 ml (19 fl oz) vegetable stock

1½ tablespoons medium curry powder

1 cinnamon stick

4 cardamom pods, crushed

1 teaspoon ground turmeric

1 teaspoon cumin seeds

For the sauce

calorie controlled cooking spray

2 medium onions, chopped

2 garlic cloves, crushed

5 cm (2 inches) fresh root ginger, peeled and grated

2 tablespoons medium curry powder

½ teaspoon ground turmeric

½ teaspoon chilli powder

400 g can chopped tomatoes

1 tablespoon toasted sliced almonds, to garnish

Biryani, or biriani, is a Persian word for a type of rice. Traditionally, a biryani dish is cooked slowly in an oven. Although rice cooked in this way does not fluff up as it does when boiled, it has a lovely creamy taste.

1 Preheat the oven to Gas Mark 4/180°C/fan oven 160°C.

2 To make the biryani, mix all the biryani ingredients together in a flame and ovenproof dish. Heat gently on the hob until simmering, cover with a tight-fitting lid and transfer to the preheated oven. Cook for 40 minutes.

3 Meanwhile, to make the sauce, heat a non-stick frying pan and spray with the cooking spray. Stir-fry the onions for about 8 minutes, until soft and brown. Add the rest of the sauce ingredients to the onions, bring to the boil, cover with a tight-fitting lid and simmer gently for 30 minutes.

4 Put the sauce mixture into a food processor or liquidiser and whizz until smooth.

5 To serve the biryani, fluff up the rice with a fork, then scatter the toasted almonds over the top. Serve the sauce separately.

Variation… Turn this into a chicken and vegetable dish by stirring in 2 cooked skinless chicken breasts 110 g (4 oz) each, cut into bite size pieces, just before serving.

Ginger and garlic fried rice

Serves 4

339 calories per serving

Takes 30 minutes

240 g (8½ oz) dried brown
basmati rice

calorie controlled cooking
spray

1 onion, sliced

1 large red pepper, de-seeded
and sliced

200 g (7 oz) pak choi, sliced
on the diagonal

2 large garlic cloves, chopped

5 cm (2 inches) fresh root
ginger, peeled and grated

150 g (5½ oz) frozen petits
pois

3 tablespoons soy sauce

3 eggs, lightly beaten

freshly ground black pepper

2 tablespoons chopped fresh
coriander, to garnish

*This substantial dish is essentially vegetarian but you can
add pork for meat eaters – see Variation, below.*

1 Cook the rice according to the instructions on page 142
(Perfectly Cooked Rice).

2 Heat a large, non-stick wok or frying pan and spray with the
cooking spray. Add the onion and stir-fry for 3 minutes, then
toss in the pepper and pak choi and cook, stirring continuously,
for 3 minutes.

3 Add the garlic, ginger and petits pois and stir-fry for another
minute. Stir in the cooked rice and heat through, stirring
continuously.

4 Make a well in the centre and pour in the soy sauce and
eggs. Draw the rice and vegetables into the egg mixture,
stirring continuously until the egg is cooked. Make sure it does
not stick to the bottom of the pan. Season with freshly ground
black pepper and serve garnished with coriander.

Variation… Add 75 g (2¾ oz) cooked lean pork strips per
person.

Indian style pilau

Serves 2
395 calories per serving
Takes 20 minutes to prepare,
  15 minutes to cook

1 teaspoon sunflower oil
1 small onion, chopped
1 garlic clove, chopped
125 g (4½ oz) carrots, diced
1 red pepper, de-seeded and
  diced
150 g (5½ oz) dried basmati
  rice
1 teaspoon ground turmeric
½ teaspoon chilli powder
½ teaspoon cumin seeds
½ teaspoon ground coriander
600 ml (20 fl oz) vegetable
  stock
50 g (1¾ oz) frozen peas
2 tablespoons chopped fresh
  coriander, to garnish

*This colourful mix of vegetables with a hint of spice is a
perfect accompaniment to grilled meat, fish or chicken.*

1 Heat the oil in a large saucepan and add the onion, garlic,
carrots, pepper, rice, turmeric, chilli powder, cumin seeds and
ground coriander. Stir well and cook for 2 minutes.

2 Add the stock and cook, covered, for 15 minutes until
virtually all the stock has been absorbed and the rice is just
tender. Add the peas and cook for a further 2–3 minutes.
Sprinkle with the fresh coriander and serve.

Tip... Add 225 g (8 oz) cooked shredded chicken for a more
substantial dish.

Chapatis

Makes 9
80 calories per serving
Takes 20 minutes +
  30 minutes resting

175 g (6 oz) plain wholemeal
  flour, plus 25 g (1 oz) for
  rolling
salt
calorie controlled cooking
  spray

Chapatis are traditional Indian breads. They are cooked very quickly on the hob so that the dough puffs up. As they are made without fat, they are an ideal accompaniment to a curry to help keep the calorie count low.

1 Place the wholemeal flour in a medium bowl and season with salt.

2 Make a well in the middle and pour in 125 ml (4 fl oz) cold water.

3 Using two fingers, gently stir the flour and water together. Form it into a ball, adding more water as required – up to 125 ml (4 fl oz). Once all the flour has been incorporated, knead to form a smooth dough.

4 Sprinkle the dough with a few drops of water, cover it with a clean, damp tea towel and set aside for 30 minutes.

5 Knead the dough again, then divide it into 9 equal-sized pieces.

6 Using the reserved flour, roll each piece out into a thin circle about 15 cm (6 inches) across.

7 Preheat a frying pan and spray with the cooking spray. Fry each chapati for 1 minute on each side.

8 Serve immediately or leave until cool before wrapping in cling film and freezing until required.

Naan bread

Makes 6

265 calories per serving

Takes 30 minutes to prepare
+ 10 hours chilling +
15 minutes rising,
5–10 minutes to cook

425 g (15 oz) plain flour, plus
  extra for sprinkling

1 teaspoon salt

150 g (5 oz) low fat plain bio
  yogurt

1 teaspoon active dried yeast

calorie controlled cooking
  spray

½ tablespoon poppy seeds,
  for sprinkling

Naan bread is traditionally served with balti dishes but is good with any Indian food.

1 Put the flour, salt, yogurt and yeast in a bowl and add up to 150 ml (5 fl oz) warm water to form a dough.

2 Knead the dough for 5 minutes until it is soft and feels springy.

3 Cover it with cling film and chill in the fridge for at least 4–5 hours or, preferably, overnight, if you have time.

4 Uncover the dough and knead it for 3 minutes; then cover it again and chill for at least 4–5 hours.

5 Divide the dough into 6 equal pieces and roll each into a ball. Flatten each one into an oval and gently pull it into a longer oval so that the dough is about the thickness of your fingers.

6 Preheat the oven to its highest temperature.

7 Lightly spray 2 baking sheets with the cooking spray and sprinkle them with flour. Put the naan breads on the prepared sheets and leave to rest for 15 minutes.

8 Sprinkle the naan breads with a little water and a few poppy seeds. Bake them for 5–10 minutes or until the surface bubbles up and starts to brown.

9 Serve the breads immediately or cool and freeze until needed.

Tips... The cooking time will depend on how hot your oven is and the thickness of the bread. Naans wrapped in cling film will keep in the fridge for one day. To freeze, wrap each one in cling film and freeze for up to 1 month.

Spicy vegetable-topped naan

Serves 2

315 calories per serving

Takes 20 minutes + more than 10 hours to make the naan in advance

calorie controlled cooking spray

1 medium red pepper, de-seeded and sliced thinly

1 medium green pepper, de-seeded and sliced thinly

1 medium courgette, cut into 2.5 cm (1 inch) batons

100 g (3½ oz) mushrooms, sliced thickly

4 spring onions, cut into 2.5 cm (1 inch) lengths

1 tablespoon medium curry powder

1 garlic clove, crushed

½ teaspoon ground turmeric

150 g (5½ oz) 0% fat Greek yogurt

40 g (1½ oz) sultanas

1 naan bread (see page 138)

salt and freshly ground black pepper

Turmeric is used not only for its flavour, but also for the distinctive golden colour it gives to curries. Serve this curry for a light lunch or suppertime snack.

1 Heat a non-stick frying pan and spray with the cooking spray. Stir-fry the vegetables for 3–4 minutes, or until starting to soften.

2 Preheat the grill.

3 Add the curry powder, garlic and turmeric to the vegetables in the pan and stir to mix.

4 Reduce the heat and mix in the yogurt and sultanas. Cover the pan and simmer gently for 2 minutes.

5 Meanwhile, grill the naan bread on both sides.

6 Season the vegetables to taste and serve with the bread, torn in half.

Tip… The vegetable mixture can either be served on top of the naan or the naan can be split in half and the mixture used as a filling.

Variation… These spiced vegetables can also be served as a side dish with a main course of meat or fish.

Perfectly cooked rice

Serves 4

175 calories per serving

Takes 10 minutes to prepare,
  25 minutes to cook

200 g (7 oz) dried basmati rice

There are many ways to cook rice but this method creates light, fluffy grains and is equally successful with various rice varieties.

1 Rinse the rice in a sieve under cold running water then tip into a medium lidded saucepan.

2 Pour in 400 ml (14 fl oz) cold water. Bring to the boil, then reduce the heat to its lowest setting and cover the pan. Simmer for 10 minutes, without removing the lid, until the water has been absorbed and the grains are tender.

3 Remove the pan from the heat, take off the lid and cover the rice with a clean tea towel. Leave to stand for 5 minutes, while the rice fluffs up.

Tips… For brown basmati rice, follow the instructions above, increasing the quantity of water to 425 ml (15 fl oz). It will take about 20–25 minutes to cook until tender. Then leave to stand for 5 minutes following the instructions in step 3.

It's useful to know that 50 g (1¾ oz) dried rice is equivalent to 140 g (5 oz) cooked rice.

Variation… Flavour the rice with 1 raw green chilli, de-seeded and chopped, 1 tablespoon of toasted coconut, 1 tablespoon of lime juice and the grated zest of a lime. It's fantastic with barbecued food.

Spiced brown rice and mushroom pilau

Serves 4

204 calories per serving

Takes 10 minutes to prepare,
 40 minutes to cook

**calorie controlled cooking
 spray**
1 onion, sliced thinly
1 teaspoon black onion seeds
1 teaspoon cumin seeds
1 cinnamon stick
¼ teaspoon ground turmeric
2 bay leaves
**200 g (7 oz) chestnut
 mushrooms, sliced**
**200 g (7 oz) dried brown
 basmati rice**
500 ml (18 fl oz) boiling water

Enjoy this spiced rice with any tasty curry.

1 Heat a large, lidded saucepan until hot and spray with the
cooking spray. Cook the onion for 4 minutes over a high heat
until browned, stirring once or twice, and adding a splash of
water if it starts to stick. Add all the spices and the bay leaves
and cook for 1 minute, stirring, then mix in the mushrooms plus
2 tablespoons of water. Cover and cook for 2 minutes.

2 Stir the rice into the pan and add the boiling water. Bring to
the boil, give the rice a final stir then cover tightly with a lid and
reduce the heat to a very low setting. Cook undisturbed for 35
minutes by which time all the liquid should be absorbed and
the rice will be tender.

3 Remove from the heat, take off the lid and cover the rice
with a clean tea towel. Leave to stand for 5 minutes, while the
rice fluffs up.

Thai fried rice with toasted cashews

Serves 1
282 calories per serving
Takes 35 minutes

50 g (1¾ oz) dried Thai
jasmine rice

calorie controlled cooking
spray

1 cm (½ inch) fresh root
ginger, peeled and cut into
very thin strips

6 cashew nuts

1 teaspoon soy sauce

2 spring onions, sliced
diagonally and separated
into white and green parts

1 garlic clove, chopped

a lemongrass stalk, chopped
finely

½ red chilli, de-seeded and
chopped

fresh coriander sprigs, to
garnish

For the dressing

1 tablespoon soy sauce

1 teaspoon lime juice

a large pinch of caster sugar

*Jasmine rice has a nutty flavour and is a slightly sticky
rice compared to basmati or plain white rice.*

1 Put the rice in a lidded pan and pour in enough cold water to
cover by 1 cm (½ inch). Bring to the boil, then reduce the heat
to its lowest setting. Cover and simmer for about 10 minutes
until the rice is tender and the water is absorbed.

2 Remove the pan from the heat. Leave to stand for 5 minutes,
still covered. Spread the rice on a baking tray and leave to cool.

3 Heat a non-stick wok or frying pan and spray with the
cooking spray. Add the ginger and stir-fry for 3 minutes until it
becomes crisp and golden. Remove from the pan and set aside.

4 Put the cashew nuts in the pan, spray with the cooking spray
and toast over a medium-low heat for 2 minutes, turning them
frequently. Add the soy sauce and turn to coat the nuts. Cook
for another minute, then remove from the pan and set aside.

5 Wipe the pan, spray with the cooking spray and stir-fry the
white part of the spring onions, garlic, lemongrass and chilli for
a minute. Add the cold rice, turning it to break up any lumps
and combine it with the other ingredients.

6 Make the dressing. Mix together the soy sauce, lime juice
and sugar. Pour the dressing into the pan, stir and heat through.
Stir the green part of the spring onions into the rice. Serve
topped with the coriander, cashew nuts and crisp ginger.

Tip… Because a stir-fry cooks very quickly, prepare all the
ingredients in advance so you have them ready. Make sure
the cooked rice is completely cold before stir-frying, and
piping hot before serving.

Saffron rice

Serves 4

225 calories per serving

Takes 20 minutes + at least
30 minutes soaking

a pinch of saffron threads
250 g (9 oz) dried basmati rice
juice of ½ a lemon
½ teaspoon cumin seeds
**4 cardamom pods, crushed
slightly**
2.5 cm (1 inch) cinnamon stick
**salt and freshly ground black
pepper**

An aromatic rice dish to serve with your curries.

1 Soak the saffron threads in a little boiling water for at least
30 minutes. Drain, reserving the soaking liquid. Rinse the rice
under cold running water, then drain.

2 Place the saffron liquid, rice and all the other ingredients in
a pan and cover with cold water. Bring to the boil, then simmer
for 10 minutes.

3 Drain the rice and transfer to a bowl. Cover it with a clean,
dry tea towel and leave to stand for 4 minutes before serving.

Tip… Covering the hot cooked rice with a tea towel and
leaving it to stand for a few minutes dries the rice slightly
and makes it fluff up.

Stuffed paratha

Makes 5

225 calories per paratha

Takes 50 minutes

❄

200 g (7 oz) plain flour, plus
  5 tablespoons for dusting

½ teaspoon salt

1 tablespoon vegetable oil

calorie controlled cooking
  spray

100 g (3½ oz) potatoes,
  quartered

1 small onion, chopped finely

1 teaspoon black mustard
  seeds

½ teaspoon ground turmeric

A delicious and filling alternative to naan or chapatis.

1 Sift the flour and salt into a mixing bowl, stir and then make a well in the centre. Pour in 125 ml (4 fl oz) tepid water and the oil. Stir with a fork until combined, then use your hands to form the mixture into a soft ball of dough. It should be fairly sticky, so add more water if the dough is too dry.

2 Lightly dust a clean work surface with 3 tablespoons of the flour and knead the dough for 5 minutes until it becomes smooth. Spray a clean bowl with the cooking spray. Add the dough and spray the dough too, then cover and set aside for 30 minutes.

3 Meanwhile, bring a pan of water to the boil, add the potatoes and cook until tender. Drain, then mash. Leave to cool.

4 Heat a non-stick frying pan until hot, spray with the cooking spray and fry the onion for 4 minutes. Add the mustard seeds and continue to cook for another 2 minutes. Stir in the turmeric, then transfer to a bowl with the mashed potato. Beat together to form a paste.

5 Divide the dough into five pieces. Lightly dust a work surface with the remaining 2 tablespoons of flour. Roll each piece of dough into a circle, about 19 cm (7½ inches) in diameter and 1 cm (½ inch) thick. Spread 2 teaspoons of the potato mixture over one half of the dough then fold into a semi-circle, and then fold again into quarters. Roll out until about 19 cm (7½ inches) in diameter (the shape doesn't need to be perfectly round). Pat off any excess flour.

6 Heat a large non-stick frying pan until hot. Spray with the cooking spray and cook the breads, one at a time, for 2 minutes on each side until light golden. They are best served warm.

Tip… Enjoy with 1 tablespoon per person of the Raita on page 27.

Pilau rice with peppers and sweetcorn

Serves 4

320 calories per serving

Takes 15 minutes to prepare,
30 minutes to cook

1 tablespoon sunflower oil

1 onion, diced

225 g (8 oz) carrots, diced

2 garlic cloves, crushed

1 red pepper, de-seeded and diced

1 green pepper, de-seeded and diced

225 g (8 oz) dried basmati rice

1 teaspoon ground coriander

1 teaspoon cumin seeds

½ teaspoon ground turmeric

2 tablespoons tomato purée

600 ml (20 fl oz) vegetable stock

50 g (1¾ oz) frozen sweetcorn

50 g (1¾ oz) frozen peas

2 tablespoons chopped fresh coriander

This is another version of a pilau with a distinct tomato flavour. Serve as an accompaniment to curry or simply on its own as a tasty snack.

1 Heat the oil in a large pan and add the onion, carrots and garlic. Cook for 2 minutes and then add the peppers, rice, ground coriander, cumin and turmeric. Cook for a further 2 minutes, stirring well so the rice grains are coated in the spice mix.

2 Add the tomato purée and stock and bring to the boil. Cover, reduce the heat and simmer for 20 minutes, until the liquid has been absorbed and the rice is tender.

3 Add the sweetcorn and peas and stir well. Cook for a further 2–3 minutes until piping hot. Sprinkle with the chopped coriander just before serving.

Vegetable fried rice

Serves 1
390 calories per serving
Takes 15 minutes

60 g (2 oz) dried brown
  basmati rice
100 g (3½ oz) mushrooms,
  sliced
½ red pepper, diced
1 small courgette, diced
calorie controlled cooking
  spray
4 spring onions, sliced
50 g (1¾ oz) frozen peas
1 medium egg, beaten
salt and freshly ground black
  pepper

*This multi-coloured, stir-fried rice dish is a great mixture
of tastes and textures.*

1 Cook the rice in boiling water for 10 minutes, then rinse in
cold water and drain well. Meanwhile, in a non-stick frying pan,
stir-fry the mushrooms, pepper and courgette in the cooking
spray for 4 minutes.

2 Add the spring onions and frozen peas and cook for a further
minute. Stir in the rice and cook for 1 minute, stirring.

3 Beat the egg with seasoning, push the rice to one side of
the pan, and pour in the egg. Cook for about 30 seconds until
almost set, then stir into the rice and mix well, ensuring that
the rice is hot.

Vegetable pilau

Serves 4
295 calories per serving
Takes 35 minutes

250 g (9 oz) dried basmati rice
4 garlic cloves, crushed
2.5 cm (1 inch) fresh root ginger, peeled and grated
4 cardamom pods, crushed slightly
2 teaspoons ground coriander
1 teaspoon chilli powder
½ teaspoon turmeric
2 heaped tablespoons frozen peas
calorie controlled cooking spray
400 g (14 oz) mixed vegetables, diced or sliced finely, e.g. red and green peppers, cauliflower florets, small brown mushrooms
2 heaped tablespoons sultanas
salt and freshly ground black pepper

A simple but delicious rice and vegetable mixture. Serve with chopped fresh tomatoes and chapatis.

1 Put the rice, garlic, ginger and all the spices into a pan and cover with cold water. Bring to the boil and continue to cook for 10 minutes. Add the peas after 7 minutes.

2 Heat a non-stick pan and spray with the cooking spray. Stir-fry the mixed vegetables for 3–4 minutes.

3 When the rice is cooked, rinse and drain it, and transfer to a serving dish. Cover the dish with a clean, dry tea towel and leave for 3–4 minutes.

4 Stir the vegetables and sultanas into the rice mixture, season to taste and serve.

Desserts

Apricots in cardamom syrup

Serves 2
244 calories per serving
Takes 5 minutes to prepare,
  20 minutes to cook

200 g (7 oz) dried apricots
3 cardamom pods, split
1 star anise
1 cinnamon stick
2 tablespoons clear honey
2 tablespoons quark, to serve
ground cinnamon, to serve

Dried apricots become plump, soft and sweet when poached in a fragrant syrup. They're also delicious served for breakfast with natural yogurt.

1 Put the apricots in a lidded saucepan with 300 ml (10 fl oz) water and the cardamom, star anise, cinnamon and honey. Stir until combined then bring to the boil.

2 Reduce the heat and simmer, partially covered, for 20 minutes until the apricots have softened and the sauce is syrupy. Remove the cardamom.

3 Serve the apricots in a bowl topped with a spoonful of quark, lightly sprinkled with ground cinnamon.

Tip... Look out for unsulphured dried apricots, which are dark golden in colour and have a toffee-like flavour.

Indian ice cream

Serves 4

305 calories per serving

Takes 10 minutes + 8 hours
freezing + 50 minutes
softening

**410 g can light condensed
milk**

30 g (1¼ oz) sugar

seeds from 2 cardamom pods

*This lovely Indian ice cream, known as kulfi, is
traditionally made by reducing full fat milk – a long
process. Using a can of light condensed milk is a faster
and heathier alternative.*

1 Put all the ingredients in a food processor or liquidiser, and
whisk or blend until well mixed.

2 Pour the mixture into a lidded plastic container and put it in
the freezer.

3 After 2 hours, remove the kulfi from the freezer and stir it
through with a fork to break up any lumps. Cover the container
again and return it to the freezer.

4 After another 2 hours, repeat step 3. Then leave the kulfi to
freeze for at least 8 hours or preferably overnight.

5 Transfer the kulfi to the fridge 45–50 minutes before serving,
to allow it to soften. Serve 4 small scoops per person.

Indian rice pudding

Serves 2

285 calories per serving

Takes 10 minutes to prepare,
35 minutes to cook

75 g (2¾ oz) dried pudding
rice

250 ml (9 fl oz) skimmed milk

2 cardamom pods, split

1 teaspoon ground cinnamon

2 tablespoons fructose or
caster sugar

finely grated zest of ½ a small
orange

3 tablespoons reduced fat
coconut milk

½ teaspoon ground nutmeg

2 teaspoons toasted flaked
almonds

*This quick rice pudding is infused with cinnamon, orange
and cardamom for a wonderful flavour and aroma.*

1 Put the rice into a heavy bottomed, lidded saucepan. Cover
with 300 ml (10 fl oz) cold water. Bring to the boil, then reduce
the heat and simmer, uncovered, for 15 minutes.

2 Pour the skimmed milk into the pan, then add the cardamom
pods, cinnamon, fructose or sugar, and orange zest. Reduce
the heat and simmer, partially covered, for 20 minutes, stirring
regularly, or until the rice is tender. Stir in the coconut milk and
heat through. Remove the cardamom pods.

3 Spoon the rice into small serving bowls, sprinkle with the
nutmeg and top with the almonds.

Banana yogurt ice

Serves 4

175 calories per serving

Takes 10 minutes + 12 hours freezing + 50 minutes softening

300 g (10½ oz) low fat plain bio yogurt

3 medium, very ripe bananas

40 g (1½ oz) sugar

2 tablespoons skimmed milk powder

This recipe is best made with very ripe bananas – it's an ideal way to use up bananas whose skins are turning black.

1 Put all the ingredients into a food processor or liquidiser, and whisk or blend until well mixed.

2 Pour into a lidded plastic container and freeze.

3 After 2 hours, remove it from the freezer and stir through with a fork to break up any lumps. Cover the container again and return to the freezer.

4 After another 2 hours, repeat this procedure, then leave to freeze for at least 8 hours or preferably overnight.

5 Transfer the yogurt ice from the freezer to the fridge 45–50 minutes before serving, to allow it to soften. Serve 2 medium scoops per person in individual bowls.

Passion fruit yogurt

Serves 4

80 calories per serving

Takes 10 minutes +
   30 minutes marinating

a pinch of saffron threads
4 tablespoons warm skimmed
400 g (14 oz) 0% fat Greek
   yogurt
2 teaspoons icing sugar
6 passion fruit, halved

This is a traditional Indian dessert – if you like the taste of saffron, you will love it.

1 Soak the saffron threads in the warm skimmed milk for at least 30 minutes.

2 Put the saffron and its soaking liquid, the yogurt and icing sugar in a bowl. Stir well to mix.

3 Add the pulp from four of the passion fruit and stir again.

4 Divide the mixture between four small serving bowls and serve with the remaining passion fruit pulp spooned over.

Ginger fruit salad

Serves 4
100 calories per serving
Takes 10 minutes + chilling
Ⓥ

This fresh fruit salad is an ideal dinner party dessert and tastes even better when it's had time for the flavours to infuse. Make it the day before, then serve it straight from the fridge.

225 g (8 oz) fresh pineapple, cubed

225 g (8 oz) fresh mango, peeled and cubed

200 g (7 oz) cantaloupe melon, de-seeded, peeled and cubed

50 g (1¾ oz) seedless grapes

30 g (1¼ oz) stem ginger in syrup, rinsed and sliced thinly

1 teaspoon sugar

juice of a lime

mango slices with skin, to decorate (optional)

1 Place all the fruit ingredients and the stem ginger in a serving bowl.

2 Put the sugar and lime juice in a small measuring jug and make up to 75 ml (3 fl oz) with water. Stir until the sugar has dissolved.

3 Pour the lime syrup over the fruit, cover and chill in the fridge for 1 hour, or preferably overnight, if you have time.

4 Serve in bowls with the mango slices for more colour and texture, if desired.

Mango kulfi

Serves 8

117 calories per serving

Takes 15 minutes + 4 hours
freezing + 15 minutes
softening

1 large ripe mango

1 teaspoon vanilla extract

400 ml (14 fl oz) light
evaporated milk

50 ml (2 fl oz) light condensed
milk

calorie controlled cooking
spray

50 g (1¾ oz) unsalted shelled
pistachios, chopped roughly

*This version of kulfi is flavoured with fresh mango and just
as delicious as the traditional variety on page 158. If you
don't want to serve it all at once, keep some in the freezer.*

1 Using a vegetable peeler, remove the skin from the mango.
Slice the fruit away from the stone, reserving a few thin slices
to decorate. Put the remaining mango in a food processor with
the vanilla extract, evaporated milk, and condensed milk – or
use a hand-blender. Whizz until smooth and creamy.

2 Lightly spray 8 x 150 ml (5 fl oz) ramekins or dariole moulds
with the cooking spray. Fill with the kulfi mixture. (You can also
use a 1.2 litre/2 pint freezerproof container with a lid.) Freeze
for 4 hours or until frozen – it will take longer in a container.

3 To remove the kulfi from the moulds, take them out of the
freezer 15 minutes before serving, then run a knife around the
sides. Turn them upside down and give a little shake to release
the ice cream from the mould on to a serving plate. You can
also place the mould in a bowl of hot water for a few seconds
to help to release the kulfi.

4 Serve one kulfi per person, sprinkled with the pistachios and
decorated with the reserved mango slices.

Mango lassi

Serves 1

221 calories per serving

Takes 5 minutes

100 g (3½ oz) fresh mango, cut into chunks

5 tablespoons low fat natural yogurt

2 tablespoons skimmed milk

1 teaspoon fructose or caster sugar

15 g (½ oz) toasted flaked almonds, chopped roughly

Lusciously creamy and fruity, this traditional Indian drink makes a delicious light dessert or breakfast smoothie.

1 Put the mango, yogurt, milk and fructose or sugar in a blender, or use a hand-held blender, and blend until smooth and creamy.

2 Pour into a tall glass and scatter with almonds.

Tip… Prepared fresh mango is available in the supermarkets. For an indulgent twist, just before serving, add a 60 g (2 oz) scoop of reduced fat vanilla ice cream.

Variation… Freeze the mango mixture to make a fruity yogurt ice. Pour it into a small freezerproof container with a lid and freeze until solid. Remove from the freezer 15 minutes before serving to allow it to soften.

Tropical sorbet

Serves 6

90 calories per serving

Takes 15 minutes + 11 hours freezing + 50 minutes softening

6 tablespoons sugar
½ tablespoon lemon juice
1 egg white
450 ml carton tropical fruit drink

You can make this with any fruit juice or juice drink, as long as it has a minimum fruit content of 40% and does not have more than 50 calories per 100 ml and only a trace of saturated fat.

1 Put the sugar, 5 tablespoons of water and the lemon juice into a small pan and heat gently until boiling. Simmer for 3–4 minutes until the mixture has reduced and thickened slightly. Remove from the heat and set aside to cool.

2 In a scrupulously clean bowl, whisk the egg white until it forms stiff peaks.

3 Pour the sugar syrup and the tropical fruit drink into a food processor or liquidiser and whisk together.

4 Gently fold the egg white into the mixture, then pour it into a lidded plastic container and freeze.

5 After 1½ hours, remove it from the freezer and stir through with a fork to break up any lumps. Cover the container again and return it to the freezer.

6 After another 1½ hours, repeat this procedure, then leave to freeze for at least 8 hours or preferably overnight.

7 Transfer the sorbet from the freezer to the fridge 40–50 minutes before serving, to allow it to soften. Serve 2 medium scoops per person in individual bowls.

Vanilla and coconut balls with mango

Serves 4
134 calories per serving
Takes 20 minutes

4 tablespoons unsweetened desiccated coconut
4 x 40 g (1½ oz) balls of low fat vanilla ice cream, softened slightly
1 fresh mango, peeled, stoned and sliced thickly

This dessert is ideal after an oriental or spicy meal and is quick to assemble.

1 Put the coconut in a dry non-stick frying pan and toast for 2 minutes, stirring occasionally, until light golden. Transfer to a plate and leave to cool for 5 minutes.

2 Take a scoop of ice cream and roll it in the toasted coconut until coated. Repeat with the rest of the ice cream. If time allows, return the ice cream to the freezer for 10 minutes to harden slightly.

3 Divide the mango between four plates. Place a ball of coconut-coated ice cream beside the mango and serve immediately

Index

Other titles in the Weight Watchers Mini Series

ISBN 978-0-85720-932-0   ISBN 978-0-85720-935-1   ISBN 978-0-85720-934-4   ISBN 978-0-85720-938-2   ISBN 978-0-85720-931-3

ISBN 978-0-85720-937-5   ISBN 978-0-85720-936-8   ISBN 978-0-85720-933-7   ISBN 978-1-47111-084-9   ISBN 978-1-47111-089-4

ISBN 978-1-47111-091-7   ISBN 978-1-47111-087-0   ISBN 978-1-47111-090-0   ISBN 978-1-47111-085-6   ISBN 978-1-47111-088-7

ISBN 978-1-47111-086-3   ISBN 978-1-47113-165-3   ISBN 978-1-47113-166-0   ISBN 978-1-47113-167-7   ISBN 978-1-47113-164-6

For more details please visit www.simonandschuster.co.uk